Skyliners 3

A JOURNEY TO ASIA

DEDICATION

To Mom and Dad

ACKNOWLEDGEMENTS

Thanks to John Wegg and Seija Wegg-Itkonen at Airways International, Inc., for their support and assistance, in particular John's contributions to the aircraft histories; Paul Morris, Airways International Ltd.; Dick Wallin; and of course, Mel Lawrence. The photos in this volume are from the collections of Mel Lawrence and George Hamlin.

Text & photographs copyright ©1995 George W. Hamlin

Series editor John Wegg

Historical research by John Wegg

Additional copy editing by R E G Davies

Design & typography by Bob Thackston, BTGraphics, Inc.

Color scans by Pre-Press Color

Printed in Singapore

Published by Airways International, Ltd.
14 Fawcett Crescent, Woodley RG5 3HU, England

in cooperation with
Airways International, Inc.
PO Box 1109, Sandpoint, ID 83864, USA

First edition 1995

ISBN 0 9525355 0 5

Skyliners 3

A JOURNEY TO ASIA

by George W Hamlin

photography by Mel Lawrence

INTRODUCTION

Today's Pacific Rim features massive and modern (read automated passenger processing) airports like Tokyo's Narita and Singapore's Changi, and is home to a preponderance of wide-bodied jets. There was a time in the not so distant past when such was not the case, however; early jets were juxtaposed with their piston and turboprop predecessors at facilities where you could observe the action in this region on an 'up close and personal' basis.

Two locations in particular stand out in this respect—Hong Kong's Kai Tak, and Haneda Airport, then more commonly known as Tokyo International. Both could truly be described as 'crossroads of the world' locations in the 1960s and, accordingly, featured an interesting blend of both indigenous and international airlines.

Of course, Hong Kong was not always a focus of international commercial activity. An early 1970s guidebook to the Crown Colony, in its *Historical Information* section, helps to set the scene with its quotation of Lord Palmerston, writing to Captain Elliot in 1841 (when China ceded Hong Kong to the British): "You have obtained the cession of Hong Kong, a bare island with hardly a house upon it. Now it seems obvious that Hong Kong will not be a mart of trade." The guidebook goes on to note, laconically, that "history has proved him totally and unmistakably wrong."

While by the late 1950s Hong Kong was engaged significantly in trade, we will see from photographer Mel Lawrence's pictures at Kai Tak that much of the development in the area with which we are familiar today had yet to occur.

The area around Tokyo's Haneda Airport, by the 1960s, when we will view it in these pages, was not exactly undeveloped, nor were the air services available there. A postcard from the era describes it well: "The front gate of Japan. About 350 airplanes fly about and tens of thousands (of) people welcome and see off, and inspect here everyday. Since it was completed in 1931, its particular atmosphere has been familiar."

One of those inspecting the premises at Haneda on a frequent basis was, of course, Mel Lawrence, whose work will enable us to revisit the location and times, and in the process, to become familiar with the 'particular atmosphere' of this fascinating place.

So, assuming that you have your passport, and appropriate visas, let us get on with the journey!

We are certainly glad that you are joining us in our continuing search for the classic Skyliners of commercial aviation's piston-to-jet transition era. As we are headed for the Orient, what better conveyance than that of a regional resident–a Cathay Pacific Airways Electra? You will be able to take a good look at those mighty Allison-driven fans as you board, but don't stray beyond the rope.

The climate at our first Far East location–Bangkok's Don Muang Airport—is not great-ly different, with regard to temperature and humidity, from our last port of call in *Skyliners 2*–Rio de Janeiro. Greeting us on arrival are both the domestic and interna-tional components of Thailand's airline system, in the form of a Thai Airways DC-3 (titles in English on the left side of the aircraft) and, behind it, a THAI Airways International DC-6B.

Contrary to what you might think, the Three's proprietor is in charge here, as THAI International is (as the dragon's head hints and as we will see later) a subsidiary formed in conjunction with another airline to operate the parent's non-domestic routes.

The US Army also has a presence, in the shape of a Beech U-8 Seminole (Twin Bonanza to the civilians).

An Oklahoma City-built C-47A, after mili-tary service this DC-3 came to Thailand as part of the fleet of Pacific Overseas Airlines (Siam) Ltd, an airline formed with the help of Pacific Overseas Airlines of the United States. In November 1951, the company was merged with Siamese Airways to form Thai Airways, and HS-POB became HS-TDD. Later registered to the Sky of Siam, a Bangkok-based regional airline, the DC-3 was retired early in the 1980s.

A 48-seat Type 761D (an Americanized Viscount with Dart 510s, similar to the Capital aircraft) built at Hurn in 1957, XY-ADF was written-off in a runway overrun accident at Akyab, a seaport in western Burma, on August 24, 1972.

A daily visitor to Bangkok early in the 1960s was a Viscount of Union of Burma Airways, operating a one-hour flight from Rangoon's Mingaladon Airport. UBA ordered three Viscounts in 1955 to replace DC-3s and these were, in turn, replaced by a sole Boeing 727.

In December 1972, UBA became Burma Airways which is today called Myanma Airways (which still uses the call-sign Unionair), and Rangoon is now known as Yangon.

In the background, several Douglas C-47 Dakotas of the Royal Thai Air Force's 6th Wing, based at Don Muang, rest between assignments.

Another foreign visitor to Don Muang is this QANTAS Super H Constellation freighter, undergoing some maintenance on Number 4 engine while in transit operating a BOAC (British Overseas Airways Corporation) sub-service between London and Sydney.

The first airline to order the 1049H 'Husky' convertible passenger/cargo model, QANTAS (founded as Queensland and Northern Territory Aerial Services) converted its two aircraft to dedicated freighters after Boeing 707s arrived in 1959 and used them to start a weekly all-cargo service from Sydney to London with ten stops in between, including Bangkok.

More RTAF DC–3s are present behind *Southern Spray*, together with a bare-metal Taiwanese-registered Curtiss C-46.

The prototype 1049H, VH-EAM was delivered to QANTAS in October 1956, and within three months had the distinction of being the airline's first aircraft to be fitted with weather radar. Southern Spray was sold in the USA as N7776C six years later. Used by Alaska Airlines and Trans International Airlines, in 1968 it was operated for a few weeks by Aerotransportes Entre Rios of Argentina and Bolivian Airways. Apart from a few months on the Biafran airlift in 1969 and '70, it saw little use and after storage at various locations, was broken up for spares for Aviation Specialties early in the 1970s.

Assigned to the 10th Air Force, United States Army Air Force (USAAF), based at Karachi, in April 1944, this C-47A was used by the Armée de l'Air (French Air Force) after the Second World War, then by the French High Commission in Indo-China as F-BCYB. In November 1951, it was re-registered F-VNAG (the Viet Nam section of the French register) with Air Viet Nam. Then, eight years later, it became XV-NIA when Viet Nam achieved its independence. By the time the North Vietnamese reached Saigon in 1975, this DC-3 had been retired for at least a year.

Next, we will make a short stop at Saigon-Tan Son Nhut to view a Hang Khong Viet Nam (Air Vietnam) DC-3. In September 1961, when Mel made this shot, few in North America had any significant knowledge of this location–a situation which would change rather abruptly in the following few years.

Ten years earlier, Air Vietnam had taken over the domestic and regional routes operated from Saigon by Air France. Early in the 1960s, the DC-3s operated scheduled flights from Saigon to Ban Me Thuot, Dalat, Hue, Nha-Trang, Phuquoc, Pleiku, Quinhon, and Tourane (now Da Nang), although few destinations were served more than once weekly. In addition, the Threes regularly crossed the border to Phnom Penh, Cambodia.

In 1959, the birth of both Singapore's own flag carrier and Changi International Airport were still years off in the future. Holding court now is Malayan Airways, one of whose DC-3s–named *Osprey*–is seen at the predecessor field, Paya Lebar.

From Paya Lebar, Malayan's 28-seat 'Dakota Class' flights served Malacca, Kuala Lumpur, Ipoh, Kuantan, Taiping, Penang (Bayan-Lepas), Alor Star, and Kota Bharu, and flew eastwards across the Java Sea to Kuching, Sibu, Brunei, Labuan, Jesselton (now Kota Kinabalu), and Sandakan.

After 21 years of reliable service, the Dakotas were retired in favor of Fokker Friendship turboprops.

Malayan Airways acquired this ex-Royal Air Force (RAF) C-47A from British Aviation Services in August 1947, and it was first registered as VR-SCO (the colonial sequence which referred to Straits Settlements). With the split of Malaya from Singapore late in the 1950s, it became VR-RCO, changed to 9M-ALO in 1959, then was re-registered 9V-BAN in March 1966. In 1969, it was sold by Malaysian-Singapore Airlines (MSA) to Singapore Air Services and a year later it was with Saber Air. After 24 years of flying from Singapore, it ended its days with Khmer Hansa in Cambodia as XU-DAG.

A 1943-built C-54A, this Skymaster went to American Airlines as Flagship America *(NC90414), then to QANTAS, from which it was leased to Malayan Airways. Sold to Air Express in 1977, it returned to the US with Basler Flight Service in 1980. Acquired by Calm Air International of Canada in 1982, it subsequently passed to Soundair and is currently flown by Buffalo Airways out of Hay River, NWT, as C-GPSH.*

From the same manufacturer (note the Douglas emblem on the tail), but with a different registration prefix, is a DC-4 named *Albatross*.

After BOAC and QANTAS became third-share owners in Malayan Airways in 1957, the company launched service to Hong Kong on September 28 the following year, using this 44-seat DC-4 leased from the Australian airline. The Four was replaced by Super Constellations from the same source a year later and, eventually, Britannias and Comets from BOAC.

Malayan Airways adopted the name Malaysian Airways in 1963 when the Federation of Malaysia was formed by the merger of Malaya, Singapore, Sarawak, and British North Borneo (Sabah). In 1967, after the governments of Malaysia and Singapore took over joint control of the airline, it became Malaysia-Singapore Airlines, but five years later the countries split apart and Malaysian Airline System was formed.

Following our stop at Singapore, upon arrival at Hong Kong's Kai Tak Airport we find a Thai Airways DC-4 Skymaster just in from Bangkok. As it is January 1959, THAI International is not yet in operation, hence the appearance of the 'Airways' aircraft outside its home country. It was a regular but hardly commonplace event then, as flight TH100 only operated on Tuesdays and Thursdays. After a leisurely night-stop, the crew left the following morning for the three-and-a-half-hour trip home.

Of more than passing interest is the colorful nose of the CAT DC-6 (of which we will see more later). A US Marine Corps C-54 Skymaster also lurks in the background.

Before C-54A/R5D HS-TSC was acquired by Thai Airways in 1957, it had seen service with Alaska Airlines, Guest Aerovías México, and Transocean Air Lines. Sold to Rhodesian Air Services in January 1962, it went to Bechuanaland (later Botswana) National Airways two years later, then to Air Trans Africa in 1968 as VP-YTY. Its final fate is obscure, but was possibly lost on the Biafran airlift.

One of 15 original production Britannia Series 102s, G-ANBJ was used by Bristol for a sales tour of North America in 1956 before delivery to BOAC on February 21, 1957. Following its last service, from Mauritius to London on October 1, 1962, 'BJ was one of many Brits stored at Cambridge. A proposed sale to Paraense Transportes Aéreos SA of Brazil in 1963 was not consummated, but in May 1965 the aircraft was acquired by Britannia Airways. After a final flight on October 13, 1970, and with 23,852 hours and 7,798 landings recorded in its logbook, the Brit was scrapped at Luton in March 1971.

Traveling to Kai Tak from much further west is one of British Overseas Airways Corporation's Series 102 Britannias. The 'Whispering Giant', as it was known, would be operated by the airline in both this 90-seat version and the longer-range 114-seat Series 300 (see page 84).

Although the Bristol Britannia was the world's first long-range turbine-powered airliner, a lengthy development process followed by unexpected Proteus engine icing problems delayed its service entry with BOAC until February 1957. Thus within two years it had become obsolescent and was quickly overtaken by pure-jets.

As noteworthy as the relatively new aircraft, however, is the expanse of unimproved real estate to its rear, dominated by the hill the Chinese call Lion Rock.

Air France's Far East services at the end of the 1950s were entrusted to four-engined propliners of Lockheed manufacture, such as this 1049G. Leaving Paris, the Connie would touch down at Frankfurt, Istanbul, Teheran, Karachi, Calcutta, Bangkok, and Saigon before reaching Kai Tak.

It would appear that the ground servicing vehicles here are either new, or well taken care of. Another item of note in the background (on the terminal building below the tower) is the entity which receives billing second only to the location.

Delivered to Air France in July 1955, this 1049G was acquired for spares use by Air Fret in 1968 and finally broken up at Nîmes-Garons in June 1973.

DC-6B N5118V served with PAA from April 1954 until March 1961 when it was sold to Loftleidir of Iceland as TF-LLB. A lease to Transavia Holland and Joint Church Aid (for Biafran relief flights) followed. It was acquired by the Fuerza Aérea del Perú (Peruvian Air Force) as FAP 379 in July 1970 and assigned to the Grupo de Transporte 41 at Lima-Jorge Chávez, but apparently was little used.

Pan American, of course, had pioneered trans-Pacific airline operations and, before World War II, American influence in the region had expanded considerably, notwithstanding the fact that we are in a British Crown Colony.

Douglas 'Super-6' Clipper John Alden is advancing the stars and stripes here past the company's local facility. Sixes were used to connect at Tokyo with 'Super-7' or 'Super Strato Clipper' service from Honolulu and the US West Coast, and to link Hong Kong, Bangkok, Rangoon, and Saigon to PA's World Airways System.

More local to the area is a Hong Kong Airways Viscount. One of several BOAC Associated Companies, HK was formed by BOAC in 1947 and had flown to Shanghai and Canton before communist forces took power in China two years later. In 1949, BOAC sold its interest to Jardine Matheson, one of Hong Kong's powerful trading companies. Subsequently, the airline operated only to Taipei, using aircraft chartered from Northwest.

BOAC revived its interest in the company, and with the arrival of 44-seat Viscounts early in 1957, the Taipei route was extended to Tokyo and service to Manila and Seoul was added. The type's reputation for reliability was further enhanced by HK's record of more than 99% regularity.

However, HK's success was short-lived as late in 1958 it was announced that the company would be absorbed into Cathay Pacific Airways, with BOACAC to become a minority shareholder of the survivor. This was accomplished on July 1, 1959.

A Type 760D, VR-HFJ was seriously damaged in a runway overrun incident at Taipei in April 1959 and had just been repaired when it was sold to Malayan Airways as VR-SEE. Re-registered as 9M-AMS in September 1959, four years later this Viscount was again transferred to a BOAC associate–Aden Airways–as VR-AAV. It was destroyed on the ground at Aden by a time bomb on June 30, 1967.

Cathay Pacific's second DC-3 (an Oklahoma City-built C-47B) flew the airline's inaugural flight to London (Gatwick) in October 1946. Sold to Foshing Airways of Taiwan in July 1961, VR-HDA became B-1409, then passed on to Royal Air Lao as XW-TAE in February 1965.

Meanwhile, over at Cathay's base, we find the longest-serving of the airline's fleet of DC-3s, nicknamed *Niki*.

Founded by an American and an Australian, Cathay Pacific Airways started charter operations in 1946 with war-surplus DC-3s. Pressure from the Hong Kong government about an American interest in a supposedly British concern led Butterfield & Swire, one of the great *hongs*, to take a majority shareholding in 1948. The DC-3 remained the backbone of the CPA fleet well into the 1950s, when CPA was proud to advertise itself as 'A British Airline with British Pilots'.

Those familiar with the wide-body-sized facilities of CX-affiliate HAECO (Hong Kong Aircraft Engineering Company) may be somewhat surprised at the modesty of the 1959 version.

Cathay had introduced DC-4s a decade earlier, in 1949, and VR-HFF was still performing capably after ten years with the airline. The dependable Four, following Douglas's demonstrated expertise with the DC-3, put many a company on the airline map, including CPA.

As in the previous views, Hong Kong's airport was clearly in a semi-rural area. Although the new Runway 13/31–which was built west of this central area out into Kowloon Bay–had been opened in 1958, a few more years were to pass before the present terminal was ready. The spot where we are standing today has disappeared under a solid expanse of newer reinforced concrete to support wide-bodied types, and the pristine hills are now buttressed by high-rises.

Skyliners 3

Purchased by Cathay Pacific in August 1954 as a replacement for the airline's first DC-4 which had been shot down by Chinese fighters the month before, this ex-Pan American and Canadian Pacific C-54A enjoyed a long life after its disposal by CX in January 1963. For a year, it was flown by Starways of Liverpool (as G-ASEN), then by Icelandair as TF-FIM, followed by ACE Freighters (again as G-ASEN). Sold to Invicta in February 1966, it moved to South Africa as ZS-IJT with Wenela (WNLA/Witwatersrand Native Labour Association) as a gold mine laborer transport. That company's operation ceased after a DC-4 fatal accident at Francistown, Botswana, and this Skymaster was broken up for spares at Bulawayo in 1973.

On a return visit in 1961, change was visible on several fronts, although 'Fox Fox' was still in good form. One notable difference is the new livery–although not yet fully defined–beginning Cathay's long-standing association with dark green. Geological forces apparently have been at work, thrusting buildings skyward, and the Pepsi Generation has arrived in the Far East as well.

Cathay had two of the successor models to the DC-4: one 'straight' Six, and a DC-6B. The former is shown here, wearing block titles, along with further evidence of the increasing population density in Kowloon.

With the pressurized DC-6, CPA was able to offer more comfortable service on the prestigious Hong Kong–Bangkok–Singapore route, and upgraded the run to a Hong Kong–Singapore nonstop night flight in 1955.

Built for PANAGRA as N90876 (one of only three DC-6s fitted with auto-feathering propellers), Cathay Pacific acquired this aircraft, its first Six, in January 1955. Sold to Air Vietnam as XV-NUD in December 1962, it had been withdrawn from service by April 1973 and was last reported two years later in a derelict condition at Saigon-Tan Son Nhut.

A Canadian Vickers-built OA-10 Canso, VR-HDH was acquired from the USAAF by Cathay Pacific in November 1946. In July 1948, it passed to Macau Air Transport Co (MATCO), and was operated mainly on the Macau–Saigon route until withdrawn from service in 1961. The following year, the Canso was sold to Trans-Australia Airlines as VH-SBV for 'Sunbird Services' in Papua New Guinea. Retired on January 5, 1966, it languished for 12 years at Port Moresby before being acquired for preservation in New Zealand and, after a lengthy restoration, it is now displayed as a PBY-5A of the Royal New Zealand Air Force at Wigram.

Also extant at the time was a Cathay alumnus, in the form of a Macau Air Transport Company (MATCO) Consolidated Canso (amphibious Catalina). The aircraft had been Cathay Pacific's first of the type, acquired for the so-called 'Gold Run' between Hong Kong and Macau, a Portuguese colony on the estuary of the Pearl River that did not open its first airport until 1995.

There was a close relationship between CPA and MATCO, and the latter company took over all Catalina operations when CPA abandoned them following the fatal hijack of *Miss Macau* in July 1948.

Note also the CX third-story operations/stores/canteen building in the background, completed in August 1959 on land to the east of the now disused Runway 13/31.

The flag carrier of Vietnam–which lacked widespread recognition in 1961–departs from Kai Tak with a French-registered Vickers Viscount 700.

The lease of two 65-seat Viscounts from Air France (which then owned 33% of VN and had replaced its turboprops on European routes with Caravelles) allowed the Vietnamese airline to serve Hong Kong in its own right–previously it chartered an Air France Super Constellation for the weekly Saigon–Hong Kong flight.

The Air France connection continues today, although the new Paris-based equipment of Vietnam Airlines is now the 150-seat Airbus A320.

A 1954-vintage Type 708, F-BGNU was one of a pair of Air France Viscounts leased to Air Vietnam for two years from January 1961. Upon its return to France, it was transferred to Air Inter. Following its withdrawal from service, in March 1975 it was moved to Habshiem, near Mulhouse, to serve as an aeroclub headquarters. It has since moved to Germany, where it is displayed at the Auto und Technik Museum, Sinsheim.

One of two Britannia 317s ordered by Clanair Ltd (Hunting-Clan Air Transport), G-APNA was delivered in 1959 in the colors of British Commonwealth & Shipping, the company's parent, and operated mostly on lease to BOAC, East African Airways Corp, and British European Airways (BEA). In 1960, Hunting-Clan merged with Airwork to form BUA. Sold to Donaldson Line (Donaldson International Airlines) in October 1967, it was operated for two years by Lloyd International Airways under lease. Stored at Baginton, Coventry, in May 1972, G-APNA was purchased by IAS Cargo Airlines in October that year and broken up.

Operating the Series 317, British United Airways offers another visiting Britannia, seen here in front of the new unfinished terminal. BUA flights were relatively frequent at Hong Kong during this era through the operation of charter services for British military forces. This 124-seat aircraft, as on other trooping flights, operated from Stansted, northeast of London.

BUA had, by the merger of Airwork and Hunting-Clan, become Britain's first major independent airline and also acquired British Aviation Services, owners of Silver City Airways. A new umbrella company for the organizations, called Air Holdings, was formed and it was this conglomerate which was purchased by Caledonian Airways in 1970. The new airline became Caledonian/BUA, then British Caledonian Airways, and was itself swallowed up by British Airways in 1987.

An interesting visitor is this US-registered, but Luxembourg-based, Skymaster. Intercontinental US, Inc, registered in New York, was a Part 45 Contract Operations-certificated carrier which shared the same directors as Interocean Airways of Luxembourg. Both companies worked in the former Belgian Congo for the United Nations.

Rumor has it that the large flag is indicative of a more than casual association with the United States, and the visit in 1961 of this DC-4 to an almost-bucolic Kai Tak suggests the build-up of an American presence in a former French colony in the region.

The ninth C-54 postwar conversion by Douglas, Skymaster NC30042 went first to United Air Lines, then to Transocean in 1956. Acquired by broker Charles Babb in 1959, Intercontinental Airways used the aircraft for work out of Luxembourg from 1960. Two years later, it was transferred to Interocean Airways and registered LX-IOF, and in 1964 it was acquired by Freddie Laker's Aviation Traders Ltd for conversion to a Carvair (Car-via-air). Operated by British Air Ferries, then French airline SFAIR, it crossed the Atlantic again in 1979 as N55243. After service in Hawaii, it is now stored at Naples, Florida.

The second Viscount delivered to PAL (on September 18, 1957), this Type 784D was leased immediately to TACA of El Salvador (as YS-06C) for one year pending the upgrade of airfields on the domestic routes planned for the aircraft. PAL's Viscounts were eventually replaced by BAC One-Elevens and three, including PI-C771, were sold in 1967 to Falconair of Malmö, Sweden. Re-registered SE-CNM, the aircraft flew charters until the company ceased operations on September 1, 1970. Falconair's three Viscounts were acquired by another Malmö-based charter firm, Skyline (Malmö Aero), in March 1971, but only one entered service and SE-CNM was broken up for spares later that year.

Finally, before departing from HKG, how about a look at a Viscount of Philippine Air Lines? This view of one on the 'Route of the Orient Star' displays to advantage the large oval entry doors of the Type 700. The more careful observer will also note the 'slipper' wing fuel tanks outboard of the Darts, as well as the US Navy Lockheed P2V Neptune in the background.

PAL's 'Radar Equipped Jet-Prop Power' Rolls-Royce service across the South China Sea between Manila and Hong Kong proved extremely popular, not least because of the airline's 'Famed Personalized Service' on the daily flights. The 48-seat Viscounts were also used on selected domestic routes from Manila, such as to Bacolod, Cebu, Davao, and Zamboanga.

Not surprisingly, other PAL aircraft are present at our next stop, Manila. Representing the airline's two dozen-plus contingent of DC-3s, PI-C128 taxies by wearing the paint scheme of the late 1960s.

Formed in 1941, PAL introduced DC-3s when it resumed operations in February 1946 after a forced four-year hiatus. Although PAL started to acquire Fokker Friendships in 1960, it would be many more years before the days of the DC-3 ended.

PAL's use of the Douglas twin for 'El Economico' services was intense. One trans-Mindanao flight, between Davao and Cagayan de Oro, had five stops in between, with most towns less than 25 minutes apart.

By coincidence, this C-47A was on the production line at Oklahoma City at the same time as the Malayan example pictured on page 10, and was handed over to the USAAF just two days earlier in May 1944. Assigned to the Philippines, it naturally became part of the PAL fleet as PI-C128. Sold to Zamrud Aviation in Indonesia as PK-ZDG in December 1969, it ended its days at Denpasar, Bali.

A DC-8-53 delivered to PAL in January 1968, Champaca was written off in a landing accident at Tokyo-Haneda on April 18, 1977, after recording 35,807 hours and 12,314 landings in its log book.

For longer hauls, including the route across the Pacific, the Philippine flag carrier utilized the Douglas DC-8, following its earlier use of piston-powered four-engined products (Fours and Sixes) from the California-based manufacturer. When the government took over the privately-formed PAL in 1954, it dropped the airline's service to San Francisco; trans-Pacific service was not resumed until June 1962.

PAL had ordered two DC-8-53s from Long Beach, but by the time these were ready for delivery there had been a change of government and the previously-promised funds were not forthcoming. Therefore, KLM purchased one of the DC-8s for lease/sale back to PAL, and eventually acquired the second aircraft.

Over at the local service terminal, Air Manila apparently had a fondness for high-winged twin turboprops, judging by what we find at Manila's Domestic Airport in 1968. *Queen of Cagayan de Oro* is a license-built Fokker Friendship, produced by Fairchild in Hagerstown, Maryland, and before a new career in this sultry climate, had spent time in the Piedmont region of the southeastern United States as the *Palmetto Pacemaker*.

    The tail logo is a *vinta*, a colorful Filipino sailing vessel used for centuries to link the islands of the country, hence Air Manila's slogan 'The Vinta of the Skies'.

One of several ex-Piedmont Fairchild F-27s acquired by Air Manila in 1967, this aircraft was retired in the mid-1970s and was subsequently scrapped.

Skyliners 3

Herald Series 215 PI-C866 was delivered to Air Manila in March 1966. Withdrawn from service in 1978, after a meager 12,400hr and 10,200 landings, it was later scrapped.

Air Manila also operated the similar, but far less common, Handley Page Herald. While nearly 800 of the Fokker product (including those built under license) were produced and its direct descendent, the Fokker 50, is available in the 1990s, only 50 Heralds were built.

However, the *Queen of Baguio* was delivered directly to the Philippine airline from the British manufacturer, without an intermediate stay elsewhere.

The airline had a stormy career, and halted flights for five months in 1969 because of a lack of pilots, aircraft, and funds. At the end of 1972, it was again shut down, this time by the government, and its staff and services were integrated into PAL. The following year it resumed flying as a charter operator (by now called Air Manila International), but finally ceased all operations in February 1984.

Filipinas Orient also operated high-wing props on its short-haul services: the Nord 262. One of several attempts to build a 'DC-3 replacement' in the 1950s and '60s, the French feederliner (*avion d'apport*) program had a moderate degree of success, with sales in the Far East and North America, as well as Europe.

This aircraft will become well-traveled, starting its career with Japan Domestic Airlines (as we will see on page 58), and finally being domiciled in Europe.

All three of FOA's Nord 262A-14s were acquired from Japan Domestic Airlines in 1968. Unused by PAL after its takeover of FOA, the French trio was purchased by American Jet Industries in 1975, which sold the three to Swift Aire. This aircraft, PI-C966 (ex JA8663, the last two digits of this registration are still visible on the nose gear doors) became N419SA, and in 1983 moved to Italy with Aligiulia as I-ALGR. It was withdrawn from use three years later, and in 1995 was derelict at Dinard, France.

First flown on August 3, 1966, YS-11-116 PC-C964 was delivered to FOA on October 27 the same year. Taken over by PAL from January 1974, the YS-11 fleet continued in service for several more years. In 1984, this aircraft was acquired by Mid Pacific Airlines as N108MP Awapuhi Kai; it was retired five years later and sold for scrap.

This Filipinas Orient NAMC YS-11 illustrates that the Philippine airlines had a rather complete collection of twin turboprops (with the exception of Convair-Liner conversions).

Along with Air Manila, FOA had been formed in the mid-1960s to offer domestic competition to PAL. The scheme was a financial disaster and the two airlines were shut down by the government in December 1973, following President Marcos's decree that PAL would be the sole flag carrier from January 1974.

While the scene in Manila was dominated by the indigenous operators, foreign airlines were also represented. A look at the cheatline provides evidence that Boeing 727 *Thanh Long* has not carried a Vietnamese registration for long.

Following a technical appraisal in 1967, Pan American ordered two Boeing 727s on behalf of Air Viet Nam which were delivered in January 1968 to replace the Vietnamese airline's Caravelle on regional routes.

Boeing 727-121C XV-NJC had been delivered to Pan American as Clipper Golden Light *on January 16, 1968, but passed to Air Viet Nam seven days later. A casualty of war, it suffered an explosion in the forward galley over Bangkok on September 5, 1973, but was repaired, only to be destroyed on approach to Phan Rang Air Base on September 15, 1974, when blown up by a hijacker.*

Delivered to MSA in July 1968, Boeing 707-312B 9M-AOT became 9V-BFB with Singapore Airlines. In August 1979, it passed to the then new Airlanka under a lease/purchase agreement as 4R-ALA. Two years later, it was sold to Guinness Peat Aviation in a contract to lease a 737 and a TriStar, and parked at Shannon for two years before being scrapped.

Relatively short-lived, as international carriers are concerned, and the antecedent of two current major Asian airlines, this almost brand-new Boeing 707 arrives at MNL bearing the livery of the jointly-named Malaysia-Singapore Airlines.

Four years hence, in 1972, the two countries would establish individual airlines, and this aircraft would be a founding fleet member of the now well-known Singapore Airlines.

Cathay Pacific's predilection for American-built equipment carried over into jets, although Boeing and Douglas were passed over in favor of Convair's 880, a smaller type more suited to the services operated by the Hong Kong-based flag carrier during the early part of the jet era. Apparently the resulting operations were satisfactory, as Cathay proceeded to add a number of used 880s to its fleet until finally becoming a Boeing operator (through the acquisition of used 707s).

The company's first 880 entered service in April 1962 on the Hong Kong–Manila–Tokyo and Hong Kong–Bangkok–Singapore routes and was an immediate success. Contemporary reports boast of 'on-top-of-the-clouds' comfort; the tinted transparencies of the windows; the blue carpeting of the cabin, with 12 first- and 89 economy-class seats; the single-stroke chime that summoned the air hostess; and the jet-age cuisine: kangaroo-tail soup, shark's fin, smorgasbord, and 'Omelette Surprise Alaska'.

A Convair 880M (officially designated as a Convair 22M), VR-HFT was built against an order from Capital Airlines which was subsequently canceled. After lease to Swissair for nine months from the manufacturer to cover late Coronado deliveries (see page 86), and storage at Mojave, it was delivered to Cathay Pacific in October 1964. Retired in April 1974, a year later it was acquired by George Batchelor's International Air Leases and ferried to Miami, then operated by travel club Travel-A-Go-Go (later called Jetaway). Permanently retired by 1980, it was scrapped at Cincinnati, Ohio, in May 1986.

Another Model 22M intended for Capital, JA8026 was delivered to JAL in July 1963, and served until October 1970 when it was retired and stored. The following year it was traded in to Boeing and ferried to Wichita, Kansas. Re-registered N5858, the 880 was sold to Aero American/Falair in November 1971, and then passed through many hands, although its use was limited to travel clubs such as Jonian Airways and Century 2000. In 1979, it was converted to a freighter and flew with Central American Airways and Profit Air, ending its days on the fire dump at San Juan, Puerto Rico.

As we shall see, the Convair 880 was a popular machine in the Far East. Preparing to whisk us to our next stop is *Yanagi* (*Willow*), carrying a sticker advertising that Japan Air Lines is the Official Airline For Japan World Exposition two years hence, in 1970.

In September 1961, with the 880, JAL was able to offer the first pure-jets on Japanese domestic routes. The flag carrier also opened its Silk Route to London in October 1962 with 880s, but these were replaced by DC-8s a year later and the type was then more at home in South East Asia.

After a lengthy sojourn on the observation deck at Manila, that PAL cabin air conditioning truck will be most welcome.

Tokyo's Haneda Airport was home to the JAL fleet, as well as host to a wide variety of visitors. Japanese civil aviation was re-established in the aftermath of World War II when privately-held Japanese Air Lines was formed in August 1951, using DC-4s and Martin 202s, with the assistance of future trans-Pacific competitor Northwest Airlines which sub-contracted the flying to Oakland-based Transocean Air Lines.

This Skymaster, one of two which launched JAL's own services on October 1, 1952, is a literal example of beating swords into plowshares, having been delivered to the US military as a C-54 in the waning days of the war, during June 1945.

Note the baseball caps of the ground personnel: white or red.

Operated by Pan American in the immediate postwar years, C-54E JA6001–named Hakuba (later Shirouma)–was acquired by JAL in September 1952 and sold to Philippine Air Lines in February 1964. Sold to the USA in 1968 as N7746, it passed through many hands and was last reported in October 1977, as withdrawn from use and stored.

An ex-Flying Tigers DC-6A, City of Kyoto *was acquired by JAL in August 1953. Following its sale in December 1965 to the CIA-sponsored Pan African Airlines, it also saw service with the infamous Air America. In December 1970, it was acquired by Singapore-based Saber Air, which passed it to Fragtflug of Iceland 22 months later as TF-OAE. On May 6, 1974, it crashed on approach to Nuremberg, West Germany, operating a cargo flight from Nice.*

With government backing, a reorganized Japan Air Lines was established on October 1, 1953, and the following February JAL inaugurated trans-Pacific service between Tokyo and San Francisco (via Wake Island and Honolulu) with DC-6As originally intended for American freight carriers Slick and Flying Tigers.

In 1961, the veteran *City of Kyoto* is operating what is now referred to as 'combi' service, with freight (which appears to be at the dimensional limit for the forklift) being loaded at the front of the aircraft, while the passengers use the elegant semi-circular boarding stairs, decked out in the full JAL scheme (complete with cheatline) at the rear. In another livery feature, note how the slogan 'Wings of the New Japan' dovetails with the airline's emblem.

Named for an overseas destination, rather than a Japanese origin city, is this later Douglas, a DC-7 'Seven Seas'. The first of any aircraft type furnished specifically for JAL, the ultimate version of the four-engined propliner line from Santa Monica was introduced on trans-Pacific routes in April 1958. Its longer legs eliminated the need for the Wake Island stop, although a call at Anchorage was necessary for flights to Seattle.

In April 1960, when *City of Honolulu* was caught at Haneda, JAL's propliners had only four more months of uncontested glory.

DC-7C JA6302 was with JAL from January 1958 until July 1965, when it was sold to Schreiner Airways as PH-SAE. The Dutch airliner was impounded at Lagos, Nigeria, in June 1968.

Fuji *was JAL's first DC-8-32, delivered in July 1960, and it remained with the Japanese flag carrier until retirement in June 1974. It has since been used as a cabin crew trainer at Haneda.*

In December 1956, as the jet age was dawning, JAL–now a well-established international airline–continued the natural progression of Douglas equipment and chose the DC-8 as its long-range jet. The fleet's flagship, named *Fuji*, illustrates a subtle change in livery, with the *Tsuru* (Crane) replacing the 'wings' logo seen on the propliners.

The DC-8s went into service in August 1960 on the Tokyo–San Francisco route, reducing the journey time to just under 12 hours, and completed replaced DC-7Cs by November that year. Proudly, JAL promoted 'DC-8C Jet Courier Service to the Orient: the calm beauty of Japan at almost the speed of sound', when Mach cruise number was not dictated by the price of kerosene.

From 1962, the DC-8 Series 30 was followed at JAL by the longer range -53 turbofan model, of which an example is *Akan* (all JAL DC-8s were named after national parks).

Even with the greater range capabilities of the DC-8-50s, JAL's US services required a stop in Hawaii on the westbound trip; nonstop California–Tokyo flights would not be undertaken until the arrival of the Super Sixty-Two. After JAL extended its San Francisco service eastbound to New York, and its London route westbound to the same city, it became (in March 1967) the fourth airline (after Pan Am, QANTAS, and BOAC) to operate a round-the-world service.

The industrial smoke in the background was a frequent feature at Haneda, and a harbinger of worse smog to come as Japan became ever more industrialized. Behind Gate 19 is the competition, in the form of a Northwest Boeing 707.

DC-8-53 JA8012 was delivered to JAL in November 1964. On August 22, 1968, in a portent of worse to come, it skidded off the runway at Hong Kong. Quickly repaired, the ill-fated Akan was destroyed when it crashed at Jaitpur, on approach to Delhi-Palam, on June 14, 1972.

Delivered to JAL in September 1961, JA8022 was sold to Cathay Pacific in July 1970 as its penultimate 880 (VR-HGF). In September 1975 it was disposed of to International Air Leases in Miami and re-registered N88CH. Subsequently converted with an executive configuration–complete with double bed–some enterprising salesman sold the aircraft to President Lennox Sebe of Ciskei, South Africa, in July 1987. Never flown after its arrival at Bisho's Bulembu International Airport, the 880 was auctioned in October 1991 for £2, and the fuselage moved by road to a mobile home site at Bonta Bay, East London, the following June.

A relatively clear day provides another view of a JAL 880 passing in review by a number of billboards which give the impression that goods of an electronic nature are native to this region.

This view of *Matsu (Pine Tree)* shows off the wing leading-edge slats, one inboard and two between the engines, plus two outboard of the General Electric CJ-805-3Bs, adapted from those of the 990 for the 880M (Modified).

JAL's fleet of fuel-thirsty 880s was retired in October 1970.

Japan Air Lines began what would turn out to be an extensive involvement with Boeing products via the 727, a type which–along with the four-engined jet from Douglas–would replace the Convair jetliner.

Six 129-seat 727-100s were ordered in January 1964, and entered service from August the following year on flights between Tokyo, Sapporo, Fukuoka, and Osaka, initially adding to the capacity of the 880s and displacing JAL's DC-6Bs and DC-7Cs. Another half-dozen 727 orders followed. All the 727s were named after rivers: *Tama* is seen here sporting an Expo 70 sticker and accepting passengers at the north end of the Haneda terminal building.

Congestion at Haneda and Japan's air travel explosion late in the 1960s dictated much larger equipment, and the 727s were phased out from 1971 in favor of 200-seat DC-8 Super 61s.

Delivered to JAL in July 1966, JA8318 was sold to Toa Domestic in March 1972 and renamed Fuji. *In August 1974, this 727-46 was acquired by Dan-Air (the first UK airline to use the type) and appropriately re-registered G-BDAN. It was destroyed on April 25, 1980, when it struck Monte Chiriguel on approach to Tenerife, operating a charter from Manchester.*

Delivered to the USAAF in March 1942, upon its retirement from military service this Long Beach-built C-47 went to Standard Airlines as NC17186 and was also flown by Pacific Southwest Airlines. Exported to Japan for All Nippon in 1955, it was retired on October 15, 1968, and is now preserved in a sports park at Miyano, Kurobe City, Toyama.

Japan's other major airline, All Nippon Airways Co Ltd, was founded in 1952 as Japan Aeroplane and Helicopter Transport Company Ltd (thus the emblem of Leonardo da Vinci's 15th Century 'helicopter' appears on the tail), and assumed its present name in March 1958, when it merged with Osaka-based Far East Airlines Co, owned by C Itoh & Co, a prosperous trading firm.

Early equipment included DC-3s, such as this example from which we see passengers deplaning in December 1959. ANA's nine-strong DC-3 fleet then operated to all but the smallest of its 20 destinations.

全日本空輸　JA5006

For local services, All Nippon Airways–in common with several other Japanese air-lines–made use of the twin Gipsy Queen-engined de Havilland Dove and the larger Gipsy Queen four-engined Heron. Shown here is an example of the former 8/11-seat feederliner, which entered service with ANA in 1953.

ANA also flew a couple of Doves formerly operated by Far East Airlines, which had also acquired the British de Havilland Rapide replacement type the same year. Besides scheduled services, the Doves flew sightseeing flights, acted as pilot trainers, and conducted aerial surveys. All survivors were retired by the mid-1960s.

Delivered to ANA (JHAT) in March 1953, Dove 1B JA5006 was subsequently sold to Nagasaki Airways and was retired in April 1968.

全日本空輸

JA 6152

A Heron 1B, JA6152 was purchased new by Japan Air Lines in January 1954 for lease to Japan Helicopter and Aeroplane Transport (renamed All Nippon in 1957) which bought the aircraft in July 1959. Sold to Toa Airways 1962 and converted to a Tawron by Shin Meiwa (see page 57), it was retired in 1967 and broken up three years later.

The four-engined model, the 14/17-seat Heron, is shown here, complete with window curtains and the distinctive shadowed fleet number on the nose, an on-going ANA tradition.

By 1960, ANA's three Herons flew on a scheduled basis only from Tokyo to the island of Hachijo Jima (Japan's 'Hawaii', 200mi (360km) south of the industrial city), and to O Shima, 50mi (80km) south of the capital; to Osaka and Sendai; and between Osaka and Kokura. But they also operated night mail services, and therefore their utilization was the highest of the four types in the ANA fleet at the time, sometimes reaching 11 hours a day.

By 1959, All Nippon–although it carried only about half of all Japanese domestic traffic–needed more competitive equipment and two Convair 440s arrived in October that year, direct from the manufacturer. These were initially placed on nonstop routes from Tokyo to Nagoya, Osaka, and Sapporo.

Note that boarding patrons are well-protected from the Number 1 propeller. And the New Year greeting on the nose by the fleet number makes it obvious that 1960 is the year of the clever rat.

Built as a Convair 440-89, JA5053 was delivered to ANA in October 1957. In September 1965 it was sold back to General Dynamics for conversion to a Model 640 with Rolls-Royce Dart engines and leased to Caribair as N45003. It moved to Canada with Pacific Western in March 1967, registered CF-PWR and named Javelin, *and crashed on September 17, 1969, in Elk Lake Park, Vancouver Island, BC, on approach to Campbell River.*

This Friendship Mark 200 was one of the original F.27s delivered to ANA in June 1961. Sold to Air Niugini as P2-MNE (later P2-ANE) in January 1975, it passed to AVIATECA (as TG-AEA) then to the Fuerza Aérea Guatemalteca (Guatemalan Air Force). Returned to the manufacturer in 1987 and converted to a Mark 600, it was leased to Sudan Airways for two years. Currently, it flies with Paris-based Air Jet as F-GKJC.

Shortly after receiving Convair-Liners, ANA made the decision to move up to turbo-props and ordered twin Dart-engined Fokker Friendships. They entered service in July 1961, supplementing Convair 440s on the busy Tokyo–Osaka route, and two months later inaugurated ANA's first international route, between Kagoshima and Okinawa, then a US Trust Territory.

One unusual service flown with the F.27 was a 'honeymoon route', between Osaka and Oita, near Beppu, Kyushu, a popular hot springs resort on Japan's Inland Sea.

The Friendship proved popular with passengers and operator alike, and a total of 25 was eventually acquired to cater to a rapidly-expanding domestic system.

Doubling the Darts of the previous aircraft is this immaculate Viscount 810. When All Nippon sought to upgrade its Convair-Liners, it also ordered Viscounts. As an interim measure, it leased two Type 744s from Vickers and these entered service in June 1960 between Tokyo, Sapporo, and Osaka, the first turboprop service in the Land of the Rising Sun.

The 65-seat Type 828 arrived a year later, and was fitted with television sets mounted on hat racks for in-flight viewing, believed to have been the first airliners to be so equipped.

With the phenomenal traffic growth experienced by Japan in the 1960s, the Viscount fleet was withdrawn by the end of the decade in favor of Boeing 727s and 737s.

One of nine Type 828s used by All Nippon, JA8203 was built at Hurn in 1961. Sold to Merpati Nusantara Airlines of Indonesia as PK-MVG in September 1970, on January 11, 1985, it was written off in an overrun accident at Ambon.

YS-11-111 JA8658 led a very brief life. Delivered to ANA in May 1966, it crashed into the sea off Matsuyama, Shikoku, on November 13 that year.

Continuing with the Dart-powered tradition, All Nippon Airways, with its extensive domestic route system, including a number of short-field situations, was a natural customer for the Japanese-built 64-seat YS-11.

ANA became the world's third operator of the type when it entered service on routes from Osaka in August 1965. This was not the first use of the YS-11 by ANA, however, as it had used a prototype aircraft for a special charter to carry the Olympic flame in September the previous year.

A total of 38 YS-11s served with ANA at one time or another and a handful of survivors was still operating in 1995, albeit with ANA's subsidiary, Air Nippon.

Although it ordered 727s on the same day in January 1964 as did JAL, ANA became the tri-jet's first Japanese operator when it leased the fourth aircraft built from Boeing in May that year, and placed it on the Tokyo-Sapporo route. ANA's own aircraft were delivered from March 1965.

The 727-100 brought jet speed and comfort to the domestic trunk routes, territory which is now the province of some of the most densely-seated 747s in the world.

Also noteworthy is the trouble taken to provide visitors to Haneda's relatively new terminal building with a good view of the activity.

This 727-81 has had many operators. Delivered to ANA in July 1965, it was sold in November 1972 to Hapag-Lloyd of Germany as D-AHLM. Although with the German charter airline until November 1991, it was leased at various times to JAT, SAHSA (Honduras), GAS (Nigeria), and Air Aruba. It is now with Blue Airlines, Zaïre, registered 9Q-CDM and named Bibi Yake.

空航覧遊本日

JA5046

天王星

Dove 5A JA5046 was delivered new to ANA. In 1965, it was sold to Aviation Services (Hawaiian Air Tour Service) as N5648V and was active until early in the 1980s.

Another Tokyo-based Dove and Heron user was Japan Air Service, known until June 1956 as Aoki Air Transport, which had been established in April 1952 to link Tokyo with Hachijo Jima, although operations did not begin until two years later.

The company made another change of identity in September 1961, becoming Fujita Airlines (its parent company, Fujita, was a hotel and restaurant chain which owned property on Hachijo Jima).

Illustrating the Dove contingent is JA5046, complete with navigational bubble on the roof of the cockpit.

Japan Air Service had acquired its de Havilland airliners from All Nippon. In a twist of fate, when All Nippon took over Fujita Airlines in May 1963, the Doves and Herons came back to ANA.

This Heron carries Fujita titles, but still wears the color scheme and emblem of JAS.

One of a batch of ex-Garuda Heron 1Bs acquired by broker C Itoh in 1960 for onward sale to Japanese airlines, JA6155 was acquired by Japan Air Service (later Fujita Airlines). It was destroyed in a fatal collision with Hachijo Fuji, on Hachijo Jima, on August 17, 1963.

Built in 1950 for Air Fleets as a Convair 240-19, N94276 was delivered as a 240-26 to American Airlines in October that year as Flagship Windsor *(later* Flagship Williamsburg). *Acquired by Fuji in 1961 via C Itoh, it entered the JDA fleet by merger in April 1964. In December 1967, it was sold back to the US and passed through several hands, eventually reaching the Dominican Republic as HI-286 with Alas del Caribe, then Aerotours. Retired at Santo Domingo in 1980, it was subsequently broken up.*

While similar in name to the previous company, Fuji Air Lines, the operator of this ex-American Airlines Flagship Convair 240, became a part of Japan Domestic Airlines in March 1964.

Founded in September 1952, Fuji operated local services from Kagoshima, on Kyushu, and between Niigata, Honshu, and Ryotsu on nearby Sado. After the Tokyo Electric Express Railway acquired a controlling interest in the company, Fuji acquired five Convair-Liners and started a daily Tokyo–Kagoshima service via Takamatsu and Oita.

While on the subject of Convair-Liners, North Japan Airlines (Kiti Nihon Kabashiki Kaisha) utilized four ex-Western 240 Dash 1s, which featured a ventral entry stair, a detail more popularly associated with the competitive Martin 202.

As its name suggests, NJA flew to cities on the island of Hokkaido, the northernmost main island of Japan, from its base at Sapporo. Japan's Civil Aviation Bureau (JCAB) denied NJA's request for a Tokyo route in 1962, but did eventually allow the company to expand by merging with Fuji Air Lines and Nitto Air Lines in March 1964 to form Japan Domestic Airlines.

Delivered to Western in December 1948 as NC8406H, this 240-1 was sold in April 1961 and re-registered JA5088 for North Japan Airlines. It crashed at Obihiro, Hokkaido, on May 29, 1965, while operating for JDA.

One of three DC3A-S1CGs (-375s), with Pratt & Whitney R-1830 Twin Wasps, delivered new to Inter-Island Airways/Hawaiian Airlines in August 1941, The Moanalua (Fleet No 9) was damaged during the Japanese attack on Pearl Harbor. After the cockpit had been set alight by a strafing Japanese aircraft, a stray bullet, incredibly, hit the cockpit fire extinguisher and the escaping CO_2 put out the fire. Repaired in mid-1942, N33606 was sold to NJA in December 1959 and after it had arrived in Japan, its new owner, ironically, complained about the metal panels which gave 'Old Patches' its nickname. It was sold in the Philippines as PI-C718 in May 1965 and operated by Southern Air Lines.

North Japan obtained this 31-seat DC-3 from an American carrier located in the 50th state of the USA, namely Hawaiian Airlines, which had converted the aircraft with main landing gear doors and the distinctive 'Viewmaster' panoramic windows configuration.

The venerable DC-3 formed the flagship of NJA's fleet from July 1957, when the airline started regular services from Sapporo to Hakodate, Kushiro, and Obihiro, until supplemented by Convair-Liners in 1961.

整備 JAMCO

空航亜東

JA5007

Toa Airways was yet another Japanese user of the seemingly ubiquitous de Havilland duo, including this Dove caught outside a hangar belonging to JAMCO (Japan Aircraft Maintenance Co, originally formed by JAL, Northwest, and Transocean Air Lines).

Toa (which means East Asia in Japanese) had been formed in November 1953 as a Hiroshima-based air taxi and charter operator. In March 1958, it became a scheduled airline and flew services to Osaka, Yonago, and as far south as Tanega Shima and Yaku Shima off the southern coast of Kyushu.

Dove 1B JA5007 was used by All Nippon before its acquisition by Toa Airways in November 1960. After use by Okinawa Airlines, it is now displayed at Shimotano, Shiobara Cho, Shioya Gun, Tochigi.

東亞航空

JA 6153

JA6153 was delivered to Japan Air Lines in October 1953, although never placed into revenue service. In April the following year it was leased to JHAT (All Nippon) which purchased the aircraft in July 1959. Toa acquired this Heron in March 1961 and subsequently had it converted to a Tawron. Retired in 1967, it was displayed at Mitsui Green Land, Arao-shi, Kumamoto for several years, but it is now believed to have been scrapped.

While maintenance inspects the non-retractable nose gear of Toa's just-acquired Heron 1B, the passenger agents are at parade rest.

Toa's fleet of six Herons was re-engined by Shin Meiwa Industry Co (formerly the Kawanishi Aircraft Co) at Itami, near Osaka, with Continental IO-470s. Designated DH 114-TAW, the first conversion flew in November 1964, and received Japanese type approval the following March. Toa referred to the conversions as Tawrons (Toa Airways Heron).

In December 1970, Toa merged with Japan Domestic Airlines (see pages 58-61) to form Toa Domestic Airlines, now called Japan Air System, which is now the nation's second-largest independent airline.

Toa's future merger partner, Japan Domestic Airlines (the result of a merger between Fuji, Nitto, and North Japan), was another Oriental user of the French-built Nord 262 for local services. It is likely that the 29-seat capacity of the 'ND-262' proved to be limiting in the rapid growth of the late 1960s, as all three were bought by Filipinas Orient of Manila in 1968, where we previously saw this aircraft (page 30).

JDA was the first non-French operator of the Nord 262, although Nitto Airlines had been the first non-Gallic customer when it converted options for the earlier square-fuselage unpressurized Max Holste 260 Super Broussard to an order for one 262. JDA assumed this order, placed one for two of its own, and leased the second production aircraft from the manufacturer in May 1965 to prepare for regular services.

JA8663 was the last of a trio of Nord 262A-14s delivered to JDA between November 1965 and May 1966. It was sold to Filipinas Orient Airways in 1968.

A YS-11-109, JA8662 Rubî (later Naruto) was delivered to JDA in May 1966 and survived the company's transformation into Toa Domestic Airlines. However, some two months before the change to Japan Air System, the YS-11 overran the runway at Yonago following an aborted takeoff and sank into Lake Nakaumi, fortunately without loss of life.

Not surprisingly, Japan Domestic also operated the larger YS-11 and had the honor of introducing the type to revenue service when it flew a leased prototype aircraft, named *Seika*, from Tokyo to Tokushima and Kochi on April 1, 1965, carrying 58 passengers.

Introduced at the same time as the Nord 262, the latter import was quickly outpaced by the local product which derives its designation from *Yusoki Sekkei*, or transport aircraft.

Apparently the JAL 727 on the other side of the observation deck is of more interest to the visiting student group than the indigenous specimen.

Had the youths attired in the white shirts been aircraft enthusiasts you can bet that they would not have turned their backs on this JDA aircraft. After all, it is the airline's sole Convair 880—named *Ginza*—and there will not be many more chances to observe it following this May 1966 sighting.

Not content as a feeder company to All Nippon and JAL, JDA moved to acquire pure-jets in 1964. A plan to lease three French Caravelles did not materialize, and instead it leased from General Dynamics an 880M which entered service on March 1, 1965, from Tokyo to Fukuoka and Sapporo.

Originally laid down for Capital Airlines, this Convair Model 22M (880) was completed in 1961 and leased by General Dynamics to Swissair for nine months as HB-ICM. Stored at San Diego from May 1962 until late in 1964, 880 number 45 was delivered to JDA in January 1965 on a four-year lease from GD. However, it was destroyed in a training accident at Haneda on August 26, 1966.

The first JDA 727-89, delivered on March 29, 1966, JA8314 was taken over by JAL on July 1 that year and named Tenryu. Ironically, it was sold to JDA's successor, Toa Domestic, in April 1972 as Kaimon. In November 1975 it passed to Hapag-Lloyd of Germany as D-AHLR, then to Scibe Airlift of Zaïre in May 1983 as 9Q-CBT.

JDA also ordered two Boeing 727s in April 1965 to service its new trunk routes connecting Osaka, Tokyo, and Sapporo. Delivered a year later, the two aircraft had an even shorter life with JDA than did the 880 as both were transferred to Japan Air Lines in July 1966, when the flag carrier took over some of JDA's network in a rationalization move.

As already noted, JDA merged with Toa Airways in December 1970 to form Toa Domestic Airlines, which is now known as Japan Air System.

With the July 1959 amalgamation of Cathay Pacific and Hong Kong Airways, CPA took over HK's routes northward to Tokyo, Taipei and Seoul, a move which would prove to be fortuitous in years to come. Showing the flag, as well as the Cathay and Douglas emblems, at Haneda early the next year is this DC-6B.

Pleased with its first DC-6 (see page 20), Cathay looked for a second-hand DC-6B, possibly the most cost-effective large piston-engined airliner ever built. Unable to find a customer willing to sell one, Cathay turned to Douglas and thus VR-HFK became its first factory-new aircraft.

DC-6B VR-HFK was completed at Santa Monica and handed over to Cathay Pacific on June 9, 1958. Entering service on June 22, Foxtrot Kilo remained with CX until it was overtaken by the Convair 880 and sold to Braathens SAFE in Norway as LN-SUB in November 1962. Nine years later, it passed to another, but short-lived Norwegian operator, called Saga (later Troll-Air), and was leased briefly to Biman Bangladesh. Acquired by Delta Air Transport of Belgium in 1972, this veteran was sold to Conair Aviation of Abbotsford, BC, four years later and is still in use today (registered C-GICD), albeit in the fire-fighting role.

Cathay's first Electra (originally intended for Aeronaves de México and first used by Lockheed as a demonstrator) was delivered in April 1959 and traded in to General Dynamics in June 1965 in part-payment for its 880 fleet. Leased briefly to Braniff by F B Ayer, the Model 188A was acquired by Ecuatoriana in 1968 as HR-ANQ. Subsequently transferred to TAME (Transportes Aéreos Militares Ecuatorianos), it was broken up at Quito early in the 1980s.

The days of Cathay's piston-engined equipment operating to Japan's capital were numbered, however, and by 1961 Electras were being used. While the airline had neither a large fleet, nor much equipment that was not categorized as 'previously owned', in 1959 it became a relatively early operator of the Lockheed prop-jet, as well as the first Asian airline to operate turboprops in this range/payload category.

Providing a nice color contrast to the handsome green machine is the bright red and yellow vehicle in the employ of a well-known oil company, which is supporting a technician between engine Numbers 3 and 4.

Cathay's upgrade to turbine status was not untimely, as by 1961 no less than nine other airlines (Pan Am, Air France, JAL, CPA, BOAC, THAI International, QANTAS, Swissair, and Air-India) offered service on the Hong Kong–Tokyo sector.

Also providing visiting Electras at Tokyo in 1961 was Australia's QANTAS Empire Airways Ltd, Australia's 'Round-the-World Airline'. While certainly an improvement in speed and comfort compared to the Connies which it replaced, the relative speed of this heavenly body versus pure-jets over the Tokyo–Hong Kong–Manila–Darwin–Sydney route may well have caused passengers on the *Pacific Explorer* to conclude that the aircraft was named accurately.

However, *Pacific Explorer* did have the distinction of inaugurating QEA's Electra services on December 18, 1959, between Sydney and Hong Kong. When this photo was taken, in February 1961, the aircraft had only recently returned to service after modifications by Lockheed to the engine mountings and wing structure. The year was also QEA's 40th anniversary, hence the discreet logos by the passenger door and on the tail, under the registration.

A Model 188C-08-06, VH-ECB arrived at Sydney on November 7, 1959. It was sold to Air California in August 1967 as N385AC but was disposed of less than two years later. After a number of owners, who let it sit inactive at Fort Worth, Texas, Ecuatoriana leased the Electra in December 1973 as HC-AZJ, and the following year it passed to TAME (Transportes Aéreos Militares Ecuatorianos), named Pichincha. Active for 15 years, it was damaged beyond repair in a belly landing at Taura, Ecuador, on September 4, 1989.

A Shorts-built Series 314, CF-CZB was delivered to Canadian Pacific in April 1958. On July 22, 1962, the Empress crashed during an attempted overshoot at Honolulu, Hawaii.

The airliners of the British Commonwealth obviously had an affinity for large turbo-props on their routes to Japan in the 1960s. As further evidence, here is a Canadian Pacific Airlines Britannia.

Now the *Empress of Lima*, having yielded the pride-of-place *Empress of Vancouver* in CPA's fleet following the introduction of the airline's DC-8-43s, CF-CZB notes its mode of propulsion on the tail above its type nomenclature.

CPA also claimed that its Britannias–with a three-class service: first-class 'Loungeaire', first, and economy–were the 'Finest, Fastest Jet-Props Across the Pacific'. Fast they were for the time. On a proving flight before regular service started in August 1958, an Empress Brit covered the 4,700mi (7,500km) between Tokyo and Vancouver nonstop in 13½ hours.

Empress of Auckland was a less-expected visitor from Canada in spring 1961 as CPA's Brits had, sensibly, replaced the Sixes on the lengthy Vancouver–Tokyo route.

However, the Douglases had served well and, in deference to their slower speed, had been equipped with sleeping berths. They continued in service on CPA's Vancouver–Honolulu–Fiji–Auckland–Sydney route until displaced by the Britannia in 1962. Their final use by the airline, later called CP Air, was on interior routes in British Columbia.

Judging by the ladder at the main entry door of this DC-6B, revenue passengers were not expected to board immediately.

Delivered to CPA in November 1956, CF-CZR was sold to Transair Sweden in January 1962 as SE-BDI Malmö. Three years later, it moved westwards, to Braathens SAFE as LN-SUM. After four years in Norway, in May 1969 it moved to a warmer climate with Brothers Air Service, based in Aden. Initially registered VR-ABL, it became 7O-ABL and was taken over by Yemen's Alyemda in 1970.

A DC-8-43, CF-CPI was delivered to CPA in May 1961 and was later renamed Empress of Amsterdam. *Sold to broker, F B Ayer in November 1980, it was stored at Opa-locka and eventually donated to the Florida airport's fire service.*

As was the case elsewhere, propellers were not long in fashion on the Canadian airline's Asian routes once 'CPA Jet Empresses', such as *Empress of Calgary*, were available.

Caught between the propeller and jet eras with Britannias, Canadian Pacific Airlines was in no great hurry to order DC-8s and its Rolls-Royce-powered examples (to match those of Trans-Canada) did not enter trans-Pacific service until October 1961.

Although the DC-8 was the airline's first pure-jet, it had placed an order for de Havilland Comets as early as December 1949. However, the first aircraft crashed on its delivery flight to Sydney (the shorter-range Comet 1A would have been used between Sydney and Honolulu, via Fiji and Canton Island), and plans for South Pacific jet service were abandoned.

In support of the Canadian contingent, additional North American presence in the Far East was maintained by US airlines, principally Pan American and Northwest. Both carriers had flown on behalf of the US Military Air Transport Service (MATS) from the earliest days of the Allied Occupation of Japan.

A trans-Pacific pioneer with the immortal Clipper flying boats, Pan American built up a strong landplane network both to the States, and within Asia.

By the early 1960s, *Clipper Northwind* was one of the more elderly members of Pan Am's fleet and relegated to all-cargo service.

Built as a C-54A, and the 36th Skymaster converted to civilian standards by Douglas, N88935 remained part of the Pan American fleet until December 1961, when it was sold as VP-YTU to Wenela (WNLA/Witwatersrand Native Labour Association). After this company halted operations in 1968, it was stored and later scrapped.

One of 13 Pan Am DC-7Cs converted to freighters by Lockheed Aircraft Service of Ontario, California, N752PA was sold in 1965 as N7524 and was then operated by Airlift International, RANSA, VIASA, and F A Connor. Acquired in 1973 by a company of dubious reputation called Fast Wings Air Freight, it was seized by the Sudanese authorities at Khartoum the same year.

Although it has lost its prime passenger status, there is a strong possibility that we would have emulated the crowd on the observation deck to take a good look at a Pan American DC-7C, although aircraft like *Clipper Rambler* were not all that unusual here early in the jet age.

Overtaken by the jets, Pan American gave some of its 'Super-7' Clippers a new lease of life as freighters, with the addition of large cargo doors in the forward and aft fuselage and a palletized loading system. Their maximum cargo load was 32,000lb (14,500kg) and they served for five years until replaced by Boeing 707-300Cs.

Between Tokyo and San Francisco, the freighter Clippers called only at Honolulu on a regular basis.

Definitely not unusual, but increasingly unlikely to be spotted in these colors for many more months, despite its *Invincible* appellation, is a splendid representation of a 'Super Stratocruiser' (the adjective referred to additional fuel capacity), all decked out in the classic Pan American World Airways scheme.

Boeing's mighty Model 377–it was the heaviest land-based US commercial aircraft in service until the introduction of the 707 jetliner–was no stranger in Japan as it had first flown to Tokyo with Pan Am in September 1949.

The Strats offered 'President' (first-class) and 'Rainbow' (tourist-class) service via Tokyo from Hong Kong to San Francisco and Los Angeles via Honolulu (and Wake Island).

Delivered to Pan American in October 1949, N1040V was traded in to Boeing in August 1960 and was acquired by Lee Mansdorf, a California-based broker. It then became Princess Everetta María (registered HC-AFS) with Línea Internacional Aérea (LIA) of Ecuador. Seized by the government, it was broken up at Quito in the mid-1960s.

A Model 377-10-26, N1030V was with PAA from April 1949 until retired at San Francisco in 1960. In February 1962, it was one of five aircraft purchased by Israel Aircraft Industries for the Tsvah Haganah le Israel/Hey ha'Avir (Israel Defence Force/Air Force) and was subsequently converted to a swing-tail freighter. As 010/4X-FPV, named Arbel, it served until struck off charge in September 1972 and used for spares.

Sistership *Clipper Reindeer* (a name applied during its Alaskan service) appears early in the same year (1960) in the later livery introduced by the jets.

Although the Strat became a fond symbol of luxury travel for passengers, not least because of the famed cocktail lounge in the lower deck, its operation was far from trouble-free. Indeed, its safety record was half as good as the contemporary Douglas DC-6/-7 or Lockheed Constellation.

The Strat's reign of glory is about to come to an end, however, as by September it only flew twice-weekly service from Honolulu to Manila, Saigon, and Singapore. Pan American's last Stratocruiser flight was operated that December, a charter from Honolulu to San Francisco.

Speaking of the new jet generation, here comes one of Pan Am's many 707s, in the form of *Jet Clipper Dashaway*. Intended for, but not taken up by Trans World Airlines, this 'non-fan' is a -331 instead of the expected -321 designation assigned by Boeing to 707-300s ordered by The World's Most Experienced Airline.

When this photo was taken, late in 1960, *Dashaway* had yet to be modified with a taller vertical fin (to improve control at low speeds with an engine out) and a ventral fin, to prevent over-rotation on takeoff.

Pan American placed the Intercontinental Jet Clipper onto trans-Pacific services in September 1959, which included the prestigious PA1 and PA2 round-the-world flights.

Delivered to Pan American in December 1959, N703PA was retired and stored at Miami 11 years later, then sold to Aviation Sales Co. Although intended for sale to Filipinas Orient, in December 1972 it was purchased by Air Manila International as PI-C7073 and leased immediately to EgyptAir, followed by a short-term lease to Biman Bangladesh (as S2-ABM). It was retired at Manila in February 1982.

Delivered to NWA in December 1957, N578 was sold to United Arab Airlines in October 1964 as SU-ANN. In March 1968, it was acquired by Danish charter company Sterling Airways as OY-STR. Retired from passenger flying in April 1972, a year later it was sold to Concare Aircraft Leasing (as N515TR) and converted to a freighter. Used by Zantop International from 1973, this DC-6B was sold in 1982 to Miami-based Bellomy-Lawson Aviation and re-registered N91BL. Since 1989, it has been registered to another Miami-based corporation, Gentry Inc (as N34C), although apparently it is no longer active.

Northwest referred to itself as Northwest Orient Airlines during this period–remember the distinctive gong featured in the airline's radio and television advertising in the 1960s? Like its US flag competitor, it used four-engined Douglas equipment and Boeing Stratocruisers on its Pacific routes before the jets.

The Boeings are nowhere to be seen at the moment, but this DC-6B is soldiering on in July 1960, providing regional connections from Taipei and Seoul with the airline's trans-Pacific flights. Just five years before, the economical and reliable Six-B had replaced Super Connies at Northwest.

Serving in a similar role is this snappy-looking DC-7C, still wearing an earlier variation of Northwest's long-lived red-tail livery. The Sevens finished their Pacific division careers shuttling to and from Tokyo and Manila, Okinawa, Seoul, and Taipei, providing connections to and from the jets operating the long over-water haul.

Northwest's associations with the Orient date to 1947, when it began charters to Tokyo for the US occupation forces, followed by scheduled service in July that year. Ironically, the airline also played a key role to establish a company which turned into Japan Air Lines, today one of NW's major competitors.

One of 14 DC-7Cs for Northwest, N293 was later converted to a freighter. Traded in to Douglas, it went to Overseas National in April 1962, then US Airways in 1964. The following year it went to Germany with Stuttgart-based Südflug as D-ABAN. Late in 1967, the Seven was sold to Air Trans-Africa of Rhodesia as VP-WBO and also operated as ZP-WBO. Withdrawn from use at Lomé, Togo, in 1970, it was later scrapped.

Delivered in August 1960, N803US was the first NWA DC-8-32 (JT4A-9) to be sold, in October 1962, to Union Aéromaritime de Transports (UAT, which later became UTA). Re-registered F-BLLC, it was leased for a few months in 1963 to Air Afrique (as TU-TBX), and two years later was converted to a Series 53 (JT3D-1). Leased to Air Ceylon as 4R-ACQ for one year from April 1972, it was sold to IAS Cargo Airlines (UK) in October 1978. However, within a month it was resold to broker F B Ayer as N53KM. After six years of storage at Miami, this Eight was broken up in October 1984.

Little remembered now–the more familiar association with Northwest's Pacific service is the 'Fan-Jet' 707–is that NW launched its jet service in the region in July 1960 with the 120-seat 'DC-8C Intercontinental, largest, finest...truly queen of the jets'. Because of its greater range, the DC-8-32 was better suited for Pacific duty than were the early model 707s and, as noted, Northwest had operated long-range Douglas equipment for many years.

Offering its 'exclusive great circle route to the Orient' between Seattle and Tokyo (via Anchorage), NW also flew Polar 'Imperial Service' from New York and Chicago to Tokyo (also via Alaska), and thus claimed the shortest, fastest flights from both coasts. On some schedules, the Eights continued on to Okinawa and Manila, or to Taipei.

Rather than build up its jet fleet immediately, Northwest chose to wait until the much-improved turbofan engine became available, then ordered 720Bs. A year later, it ordered the first five of more than 40 Boeing 707-300Bs to replace its DC-8s and thus became the nation's first operator of an all-fan jet fleet.

This 707-351B is one of the original five aircraft which were built, at NW's request, with a forward cargo door and space for 10,000lb (4,500kg) of cargo on the left side of the forward cabin, replacing seven rows (14 seats) on that side. The passengers sitting on the right side were partitioned off from this extra-capacity cargo 'hold'.

The 707-351Bs were introduced on trans-Pacific services in July 1963, and were followed by 707-351Cs, operated either as combis–typically in a four-pallet, 102-seat configuration–or as passenger aircraft.

After eight years with NW, N352US was sold to Cathay Pacific as VR-HGI, entering service on February 15, 1972. In December 1977, it was sold to Laker Airways and re-registered G-BFBZ. Following's Laker's demise, it was parked at Lasham, then broken up.

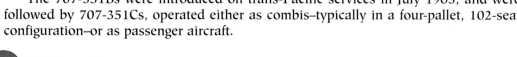

Seaboard World Airlines CL-44D-4 N229SW was leased for two months to Flying Tigers late in 1965. A lease-purchase to Transglobe as G-AWOV fell through when the UK airline collapsed in November 1968, and the aircraft was re-registered N429SW and leased to Trans Mediterranean Airways until February 1970. SWA assisted another UK cargo company, Tradewinds Airways, to get started and G-AWOV was restored to the British register in June 1970. Acquired by Transvalair of Switzerland in December 1977 (as HB-IEO), it passed to United African Airlines in Libya (registered 5A-DGE) two years later. It was withdrawn from use at Tripoli by the end of 1980.

Presaging a future cargo airline merger is this CL-44, owned by Seaboard World Airlines. The swing-tail turboprop is on lease to future partner (and surviving carrier, at least in that amalgamation) Flying Tigers. The latter company owed its colorful name to its founder's association with the group of American pilots of the same collective name, under the command of General Claire Chennault, who assisted the Chinese forces during World War II.

The Flying Tiger Line also had a fleet of its own CL-44s, which it hoped would achieve an economic breakthrough in cargo operations because of the Britannia derivative's greater speed, range, and capacity, plus reduced ground times using the swing-tail feature. But nothing could compete with the productivity of the pure-jets, and only 39 CL-44s were built by the Canadair Division of General Dynamics.

CIVIL AIR TRANSPORT 民航空運公司

As its cable address–CLAULT–hinted, Civil Air Transport was another airline with Chennault connections. Founded on the mainland after World War II, CAT decamped to the island of Formosa with Chiang Kai-shek's forces after the communists came to power and was secretly purchased by the US Central Intelligence Agency in 1950.

Apart from providing a secure source of air transport for the CIA's clandestine missions in the Far East, CAT functioned as a normal airline and began scheduled international flights from Taipei to Bangkok and Tokyo in December 1951. From September 1952, its fleet was headed by a pair of DC-4s, one of which is seen operating the Taipei-Okinawa-Tokyo-Seoul run early in 1960.

CAT acquired this ex-Philippine Air Lines C-54A in 1947 and operated it until 1965. The Four's final fate is unrecorded, but it is believed to have been scrapped.

One of the last DC-6s built, B-1006 was acquired for CAT by Asian Aeronautical Co, a subsidiary of CAT Inc (a company renamed Air America in 1959). It arrived at Taipei in October 1958 and entered service on CAT's international routes on the 15th of that month. In 1968, it passed to Royal Air Lao as XW-PFZ, and eventually found its way to Southern Air Transport as a freighter, registered N93459. Ten years later, it was acquired by Trans Continental Airlines, and since 1987 this DC-6B has flown with Air Atlantique in the UK as G-SIXC, named Jimmy The One.

From 1958, CAT's flagship for its premier–and much appreciated–passenger services was a DC-6B, complete with the airline's colorful five-toed dragon (representing China's continuing quest for knowledge) and 'Fiery Pearl' livery with the legend 'The Mandarin Flight'.

Stewardesses, dressed in traditional *chi-pao* or *cheongsam* uniforms, looked the part, too, and the luxurious service on board offered by 'The Friendly Airline' became a favorite with passengers throughout the Orient.

In July 1961, CAT introduced the regionally popular Convair 880, although it only operated a single example, and 'The Mandarin Jet' replaced the Fours and Sixes on the prime Taipei–Tokyo sector.

While touted by the airline's advertising department as 'Unmatched in Design and Speed, Ultimate in Safety and Comfort, Unsurpassed in Service and Hospitality, and Unique in Chinese Decor', not many would consider the jet's external livery an improvement over that of its piston-powered predecessors.

The interior, however, was like an Oriental palace, lavishly decorated in red, gold, and black, accented by Chinese motifs and symbols in gold and bronze on curtains, fabrics, and paneling, with authentic-styled 'moongate' cabin partitions and decorative panels above the windows depicting the legendary travels of Confucius.

Skyliners3

CAT's Model 22M (the first M delivered to an airline) was acquired in 1968 by the region's premier 880 operator, Cathay Pacific, and registered VR-HGA. Another acquisition by IAL of Miami (as N48059), this aircraft continued to operate in familiar territory under the titles of Orient Pacific Airways and Airtrust Singapore. It was leased to Gulf Air in 1976, operated for Air Malta in 1977, then returned to Singapore. Retired from service on January 31, 1981, it was broken up at Seletar, Singapore, in June 1984.

The first 707-138, flown on March 20, 1959, VH-EBA was with QANTAS for eight years, and was then sold to Pacific Western as CF-PWV. In October 1978, it was acquired by Tigerair, re-registered appropriately as N138TA, and converted with an executive interior. After two more US owners, it now flies for the Royal Embassy of Saudi Arabia, registered HZ-123.

QANTAS Boeing 707s began to serve Haneda in November 1961, replacing Electras and reducing the total journey time by 5hr 20min to just less than 17 hours. To provide additional range in the original -100 series, Boeing created the unique 707-138 for the Australian carrier, coming up with a 707 which was 2ft (0.61m) shorter than the 'little brother' 720. The first of the turbo-fan-powered -138Bs arrived in Sydney in August 1961 and, like American Airlines, QANTAS returned all seven of its original -138s to the manufacturer for conversion to the new standard.

Derived from the Latin word *vannus*, meaning fan, QANTAS introduced the V-jet designation (together with a new color scheme) late in 1961 to advertise the superiority of its 707Bs over the aircraft of all other international airlines then serving the Australian market. The symbol became familiar to millions of travelers until it was phased out in mid-1971 with the delivery of the airline's first 747.

QEA's later 707-300s were all fan-powered to start with and equipped with main deck cargo doors, making them -338C convertibles. Common combinations were 20 first- and 84 economy-class passengers plus freight; or 165 single-class seating. Like the short-bodied 707s, they were also individually named after Australian cities.

In 1966, the young *City of Townsville* stands ready for another load of freight for that forward cargo compartment. Note that the ground handling is courtesy of pool partner airline, BOAC.

Accepted by QANTAS in March 1965, VH-EBO was sold to Singapore Airlines in November 1973 as 9V-BFN. In February 1981, it was acquired by Miami-based International Air Leases, re-registered N4225J, and leased to IAL's associated company, Arrow Air, named Miss Kentucky. *Since October 1983, it has been registered in Nigeria as 5N-ARQ; most recently with Dairo Air Services (DAS Air Cargo), a company with offices near London-Gatwick but an operations base at Entebbe, Uganda.*

One of the first two Comet 4s handed over to BOAC, G-APDC made the historic first scheduled trans-Atlantic commercial turbojet service, between London and New York, on October 4, 1958 (thus beating the Boeing 707 to that honor by just three weeks). Passed to Malaysian Airways seven years later as 9M-AOC, it was again re-registered (as 9V-BAT) with the formation of the new Malaysia-Singapore Airlines in December 1966. With Dan-Air, the last commercial operator of the Comet, from 1969 until 1973, its life ended at the hands of the scrapper at Lasham in April 1975.

For a while, in Tokyo it was possible to see the direct descendent of the pioneer of the civil jet age in the form of BOAC's Comet 4. After attaining pride of place in October 1958, by operating the first scheduled trans-Atlantic pure-jet passenger service, the latter-day Comets were switched to Britannia routes where nonstop range was not as great a concern, including the multi-stop services to the Far East.

In 1960, the range capabilities of the 747-400 were a long way off indeed.

Where range did matter to BOAC, such as the trans-Pacific route from San Francisco to Tokyo and Hong Kong, via Honolulu and Wake Island, the British long-haul airline relied on Britannia 310s–at least until Rolls-Royce-powered 707s came into the fleet in force.

As with the smaller Series 100 (see page 13), service entry of the type was delayed because of engine icing problems and the model did not fly a revenue service until December 1957, between London and New York. The long-range Britannias flew west-bound from London for more than 24 hours (crossing the International Date Line, thus making two and a half days elapsed time) to link up with eastbound Comets in Hong Kong, completing BOAC's round-the-world service.

A Series 312 built at Filton, G-AOVT was delivered to BOAC at London-Heathrow on January 1, 1959. In September 1963, it became Enterprise, *the first Britannia acquired by British Eagle, and passed on to Monarch Airlines in May 1969. After operating its last passenger flight on October 13, 1974, its cabin was stripped to carry freight for Invicta Airlines until March the following year when it was retired. Fortunately, Monarch donated 'VT to the Duxford Aviation Society and it is displayed to the public at the Cambridgeshire airfield.*

During its nine-year career with the Swiss national air-line, HB-IBO was also named Canton de Vaud, Bern, *and* Solothurn. *From October 1962 until May 1963 it was leased to Finlantic as OH-DCB, then acquired by Olympic in May the following year as SX-DAM Isle of Crete,* later Isle of Lesvos. *Purchased by Concare Aircraft Leasing in August 1972 and re-registered N111AN, it had a brief spell in Canada before going to Rosenbalm Aviation. In 1975 it became tanker No 46 with Sis-Q Flying Service (later Macavia), and was acquired by T&G Aviation in February 1991. More recently, it has been advertised for sale.*

Tokyo was a popular destination for other European airlines as well and, during the piston-to-jet transition period, one of the niceties of life was that you could visit the local airport and see both the new jets and your favorite classic propliners, such as this unmistakably Swiss DC-6B.

Alternating with DC-7Cs, the Sixes serviced the Zürich–Geneva–Athens–Beirut–Karachi–Bombay–Bangkok–Manila (or Hong Kong)–Tokyo route. A banker leaving Switzerland on Friday afternoon would arrive in the Japanese capital on Sunday evening, but probably in no condition for an early morning meeting on Monday.

Reflecting a continued Swissair tradition of assigning national place names to members of its fleet, the appellation *Luzern* now resides on an Airbus A310-300.

While the more familiar association between Convair jetliners and the Swiss national airline involved the 990 Coronado, Swissair also leased a pair of 880s from the manufacturer before the delayed arrival of the longer-lasting type.

Described by Convair as 'the medium-range airplane with long-range capabilities', the 84-seat 880M was a spirited performer, with a cruising speed of Mach 0.82 (590mph/950km/h). Swissair's cabin retained the original Capital interiors and included a lounge as well as two passenger sections.

Although only operated on Swissair's Far East routes from August 1961 until May 1962, this will not be this aircraft's last visit to the area.

As noted on page 24, this 880M became VR-HFT with Cathay Pacific in October 1964, and ended its life at Cincinnati, Ohio, nearly 22 years later.

Lufthansa's D-ALAN was converted to a freighter in 1960 (named Neckar), and leased to World Airways as N45512 from 1962 to 1964. Sold to Air Venturers in the USA in 1966 as N179AV, this 1649A returned to European routes during a five-month lease to Trans Mediterranean Airways. After passing through a host of US owners, but adding little flying time in its log book, N179AV was acquired by Maine Coast Airways in 1986 and, re-registered N974R, remains stored at Sanford, Florida.

Before launching jet operations to the Orient, German flag carrier Lufthansa flew elegant Lockheed 1649As–which it dubbed 'Super Stars'–on its Bangkok service, inaugurated in November 1959, which was extended via Hong Kong to Tokyo in 1961. As this photo was taken in April 1960, just a month before the Starliner was ferried to the United States for conversion into a freighter, and nine months before LH started service to Tokyo, it appears that D-ALAN is visiting Haneda on a non-scheduled flight.

Lufthansa used a number of seating configurations on its Super Stars, including one deluxe layout for just 20 seats, plus eight first-class passengers, plus berths and a lounge, for its 'Senator' service to New York.

Displaced from the North Atlantic routes by Boeing 707s in 1960, the Starliners carried on in the freight role and as domestic back-up aircraft until early in 1966.

Berlin is not heading for its namesake destination, which would not become accessible to Lufthansa for a couple of decades, but is being prepared for departure from Haneda to Frankfurt, via Hong Kong, Bangkok, Calcutta, Karachi, Cairo, and Rome.

The boarding ramp at the forward door of this 148-seat, two-class 707 Intercontinental Jet (a Rolls-Royce-powered variant) is indicative of a common practice at international stations far from an operator's home base, namely, the use of the local airline as a servicing and handling agent.

Lufthansa's second 707-430, D-ABOC was delivered in March 1960 and, apart from occasional leases to subsidiary Condor, remained in the LH fleet until sold to Janco Panama (US-registered as N64739) in June 1977. It was then converted to a freighter and used by Air Trine and Intercontinental Air. In 1979, it was registered in Libya as 5A-CVA with United African Airlines, but appears to have been little used and it quickly became a spares source at Tripoli.

Originally built as a 1049C and upgraded later to a 1049E, then a 1049G, F-BGNG was converted to a freighter in 1960. Sold by Air France to René Meyer's CATAIR in 1968, it was flown both as a passenger and as a freight aircraft until withdrawn from use late in 1972. Acquired by Air Fret as a source of spares, it was scrapped at Nîmes-Garons in 1979.

Air France, on the other hand, appears to be using a non-airline entity to accomplish the same purpose with this Connie. That large 'G' on the forward fuselage is a reminder that when these airliners were new, their owners/operators (usually the same organization in those days) wanted to make very sure that the public, who was able to see them, knew that this was a Super G— not a C, an H, or, perish the thought, *only* a Super Constellation.

Then (in 1959) 'The World's Largest Airline' (in terms of unduplicated route miles–more than 329,000km or 204,000mi), with the 'World's Most Modern Airfleet', Air France was the largest Constellation operator outside the USA, and also the only non-US airline to operate all four basic models (49, 749, 1049, and 1649).

Like its German neighbor during this period, Air France also brought the last of the Connie line to Tokyo. While the Super Gs operated on the multi-stop 43-hour 'Eastern Epicurean' services via The Silk Road, the 1649As served the *Route Polaire*, inaugurated by the type on April 10, 1958. The 'Super Starliners' paused only for a technical stop in Anchorage in each direction between Paris and Tokyo, reducing the eastbound en route time to 30 hours. Accommodation on these flights was four berths, 16 sleepers, and 34 tourist-class seats.

But their moment of glory was brief, and the last Over the Pole propliner service left Paris in October 1960. Nevertheless, their legacy lives on as the flight numbers (AF270/272) remain the same for today's Boeing 747-400s.

Lafayette also wears both the name and *Tsuru* emblem of JAL, reflecting the then new joint service operated between France and Japan by the two airlines.

The first 1649A delivered to Air France, F-BHBK spent 19 months with Air Afrique as TU-TBB early in the 1960s. Retired at Paris-Orly on November 2, 1963, the Starliner was scrapped in 1967 although its fuselage served as a fire service trainer for another 13 years.

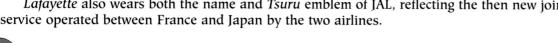

A 707-328, F-BHSE served with Air France from March 1960 until sold to US broker Charlotte Aircraft in March 1978. Two months later, it was acquired by the Tsvah Haganah le Israel/Hey ha'Avir (Israel Defence Force/Air Force) as 116/4X-JYW.

The Air France/JAL joint service on the Polar route started on February 16, 1960, with 707s, as indicated by the titles on *Château de Rambouillet*, although, as we have seen, Super Starliners covered for the new jets on occasion.

Sufficient servicing personnel are apparently present at Tokyo International's Gate 10 this summer afternoon to meet Flight AF/JL 272 from Paris and allow it to depart, on schedule, at 2100 tonight, via Anchorage and Hamburg.

Japan Air Lines was able to take over the service on June 6, 1961, with its own DC-8 equipment which operated via Copenhagen and London to Paris.

Only two Air France 707 services a week were operated to Tokyo jointly with JAL, as is indicated by the arrival from Paris of the almost-new (and unmodified) *Château de Chenonceaux* in March 1960. Over the Silk Road, five or seven stops were made with the 707s.

Air France's Boeing 707 Intercontinentals were named after celebrated French chateaux. Fitted with 32 first- and 90 economy-class seats and offering three and a half times the seat-mile productivity of a Super Starliner, the four-engined jets quickly assumed service to 47 cities on five continents. The chateaux in the sky also boasted a 'Promenade Bar' for first-class passengers, with French hospitality dispensed by four stewards and two hostesses.

Another 707-328, F-BHSD led an uncomplicated life with Air France from January 1960 until March 1976, when it was broken up at Paris-Orly.

One of the last DC-7Cs built, PH-DSM was delivered to KLM in September 1958 and sold to Südflug, West Germany, in February 1964 as D-ABAD. In 1968, it was acquired by Hank Warton's infamous North American Aircraft Trading Corp ('Biafran Airways') for use on arms and aid supply flights from Lisbon to Biafra, and used the dubious registrations 5T-TAD, then VR-BCY. The notorious Uli-Ihiala 'airstrip' (a section of the Onitsha to Aba main road), claimed the Seven in a crash on December 7, 1968.

Before the arrival of its DC-8 fleet, KLM–Royal Dutch Airlines–was one of a number of European airlines to use the Seven Seas model of the DC-7 (note the bold delineation on the tail) on its long-haul services. The commercial relationship between The Flying Dutchman (*De Vliegende Hollander*)–the 'World's First Airline'–and the manufacturer was long and productive, spanning the entire Douglas Commercial range from the DC-2 to the last aircraft–the DC-10.

Apparently the Number 4 engine of *Coral Sea/Koraalzee* (appropriately, KLM named its DC-7Cs after seas of the world) could stand to be idle for a while before heading back to Amsterdam over the North Pole via Anchorage. KLM opened this route in November 1958, which cut the journey time almost in half, to 30 hours. And, if a traveler was so inclined, he could travel around the world by KLM in less than 73 hours.

The later 'barber pole' livery applied to *Mediterranean Sea/Middellandse Zee* omits the prominent reference to equipment type, probably because its adoption coincided with the introduction of jets in the airline's fleet.

Judging by the appearance of the engine cowlings, oil consumption was a common concern for all KLM Seven Seas on the twice-weekly Polar route, which continued on from Tokyo to Biak, the largest of the Schouten Islands off the west coast of New Guinea, and still under Dutch stewardship before eventual transfer to Indonesian sovereignty.

After payment of a modest additional charge ($85), first-class passengers could secure a 'DeLuxe SleepAir berth' on the propliner, making it 'A Treat to Go Dutch'.

With KLM from August 1957 until October 1962, when it was transferred to Martin's Air Charter, PH-DSK was sold to Modern Air Transport in May 1965 as N383M. Three years later, it went to Golden Odyssey (a travel club), but was repossessed by MAT a few months later. After some time in storage at Ft Myers, Florida, it was broken up.

Delivered to KLM in August 1960, on October 29, 1961, PH-DCE was damaged at Lisbon when it hit the approach lights, but survived to be leased to PAL in March 1970 as PI-C829 (later RP-C829). Broker F B Ayer took charge of fuselage number 87 in October 1978 (as N833DA) but it found no takers and it was parked at Marana, Arizona, until 'parted out' by Evergreen International in 1984.

The paint scheme did not look at all bad on a 'Royal 8 Intercontinental Jet' either, as evidenced by this well-lit portrait of a Series 32. Reflecting the international outlook of this long-time trading nation, the aircraft is named for the American Thomas Alva Edison, one of a series honoring inventors and technologists.

Although there were no berths, KLM's advertising claimed that the Eights, its first pure-jet airliners, 'added to travel comfort' (from October 18, 1960) on the rather grueling 'Golden Circle Service' from Amsterdam which hopped to Japan via Frankfurt or Zürich, Rome, Beirut or Cairo, Karachi, Calcutta or Delhi, Bangkok, and Manila.

The consortium headquartered in Sweden, SAS, also operated the Seven/Eight combination to Tokyo during the same period. *Halvdan Viking* carries a similar '7C' device on the tail, but it cannot match the height of its Dutch compatriot.

Like its older colleague KLM, Scandinavian Airlines System also offered up to 24 first-class passenger sleepers–called 'Royal Viking de luxe Dormettes'–on its Seven Seas, besides tourist (or 'Globetrotter') service for the 33 seats up front.

As it had pioneered the Polar Route to the United States three years earlier, it was only fitting that the airline of the Vikings repeated the performance with the 'North Pole short-cut' to Tokyo in February 1957.

The connection between West and East was a completely new alternative for travelers–claimed as the first new commercial route for a thousand years.

Delivered to SAS in August 1956 direct from Santa Monica, SE-CCA was relegated to Scandinavian routes when Caravelles and DC-8s took over, then withdrawn from use at Copenhagen-Kastrup where it was broken up in January 1968.

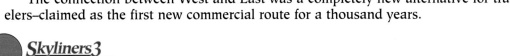

Operated by SAS from July 1960 until December 1968, this DC-8-32 (modified later to a -33) returned to the USA with United as N8258U and joined the Friendly Skies on February 25, 1969. Retired from passenger service in March 1974, it was converted to a freighter and leased to Rosenbalm Aviation between September 1975 and June 1980. It was then sold to Canadian start-up Swiftair Cargo as C-GSWQ and, after this company's demise, it was acquired as HI-413 by Aeromar of the Dominican Republic in March 1983 . Stored at Miami from October 1985, it was broken up 15 months later.

On the other hand, the Scandinavian consortium obviously did not think that, just because the mode of propulsion changed, it should stop promoting equipment types, witness the 'DC-8' and Douglas emblem on the tail of *Bue Viking*, advertised at the time by the airline as a 'DC-8C Jet Express'.

Fitted with 28 first- and 92 economy-class seats, DC-8-32s inaugurated Copenhagen–Tokyo trans-Polar service on October 11, 1960, initially on a twice-weekly 16½-hour schedule–a saving of 13 hours over that of the Seven Seas.

Seven years later, SAS and a later model of the Eight pioneered yet another route, the 'Trans Asian Express' from Copenhagen to Bangkok, via Tashkent, a saving of seven hours, and the combination went on to cut four-and-a-half hours off the polar route flying time when traffic via Moscow was allowed.

REAL-Aérovias first used Lockheed propliners for its fortnightly service across the Pacific, which started in May 1960, as is shown in this evocative scene. Note that the 'Super H' legend, denoting the model of Constellation, appears in four different places on this side of the aircraft alone.

REAL's trans-Pacific service originated in São Paulo and operated to Tokyo via Rio de Janeiro, Manaus, Bogotá, Mexico City, Los Angeles (overnight stop), Honolulu, and Wake Island .

Do you suppose the three *paulista* crew members (with possibly a stray *carioca*?) leaving the aircraft after the long grind across the ocean (named by 16th Century Portuguese navigator Magellan) might find a different color uniform a little more practical?

Transferred to VARIG in August 1961, this 1049H returned to the USA in 1969 as N566E. Acquired by S Muhammed of Temple 2 of the Holy Nation of Islam, Inc, in August 1973, it was damaged beyond repair a month later, on September 24, in a landing accident at Gary, Indiana.

This DC-6B joined REAL in February 1961 after service with SAS from 1952 as SE-BDP, named Brage Viking *then* Leif Viking. *Taken over by VARIG, it was one of five sold in 1968, to the Fôrça Aérea Brasileira (Brazilian Air Force) and was destroyed in a crash at Manaus on April 28, 1971.*

REAL's 'Super' DC-6B is indicative of the fascination with equipment promotion that was a worldwide phenomenon during the halcyon days when any airline worth its salt operated 'four-engined equipment'. Note the upper windows, for the first-class patrons in the sleeping berths.

Founded in 1946, by late in the 1950s Rêdes Estaduais Aéreas Limitada had grown, through the acquisition of, or merger with, no less than 14 airlines, to become *'The Largest Airline of South America'*, servicing more than 170 cities. Acquired by VARIG in 1961, the airline's 'Luxurious Radar Equipped Super-H Constellations' gave way to Douglas equipment before trans-Pacific service was stopped by the new owners.

Constellations also found favor with Koreanair (Korean National Airlines), which used a veteran Model 749A, the only one of its type to be carried on the Korean register. Hard to believe now, with its successor enjoying a worldwide presence, was that around 1960, the flag carrier of the Hermit Kingdom was not well known, and Tokyo was one of its two international destinations, although apparently served on an irregular basis.

Formed in 1926 (as Korean Aviation Co), KNA became the name when the government took over the airline in May 1947. Under American influence in the 1950s, not least because of a close relationship with Civil Air Transport, the company was taken over in March 1962 by Korean Air Lines (KAL), now known as Korean Air.

Built for KLM, this Constellation was used by Capital Airlines, BOAC, and Transocean before its acquisition by Korean National Airlines late in 1959. Sold to Aero-Transport as OE-IFE in October 1962, it was impounded at Amsterdam from 1964 until broken up two years later.

Air-India's VT-DIM passed to the Indian Air Force in December 1961, then to the Indian Navy 15 years later. Damaged beyond repair in a taxiing accident at Bombay on January 12, 1983, it is now believed to have been broken up.

Air-India operated the Lockheed 1049G extensively, acquiring five of them, including *Rani of Ayodhya*, to supplement two C and three E models. The Super Connies completely replaced the earlier 749/749As in 1958, but lasted only four years. All were named after ranis–Hindu rajah's wives.

Operating over 'The Route of the Magic Carpet', the Connies left Bombay early in the afternoon and arrived at Tokyo late in the afternoon of the following day, as seen here. The thrice-weekly schedule must give pause to the claim that the journey was 'Swift Super Constellation Luxury', although for those fortunate to travel in the back of the bus, first-class offered 'Every Seat a Slumberette'.

Early jet operations by aviation pioneer J R D Tata's renowned flag carrier were entrusted to Rolls-Royce-powered Intercontinental Boeing 707s such as *Everest*, seen here getting under way from Tokyo to Bombay, via Hong Kong, Bangkok, and Calcutta.

Even though the airline had entered a new age of transport–and became an all-jet airline in 1962–it took pains to proclaim in its advertising that it was 'The Jet Airline That Treats You Like a Maharajah' with saris, stewards, service, and smiles in the cabin.

Air-India's famous little Maharajah character was conceived by commercial director 'Bobby' Kooka, and brought to life by artist Umesh Rao. Thought to be out of tune with the jet age, it was discarded when the airline's 'old guard' retired.

Boeing 707-437 VT-DJK was Air-India's third of an original order for 707s placed on August 31, 1956, and delivered in March 1960. It was retired and stored at Bombay in April 1980.

The 238th DC-6, HS-TGD was delivered to SAS in May 1952 as OY-KMA Torkil Viking and leased to THAI International between March 1961 and November 1962. Syrian Arab Airlines purchased this DC-6B in March 1964 as YK-AED, and retired it at Damascus by 1979.

Coming from the same direction, but not as far, is a DC-6B of THAI International. Any connection between the Viking longship livery and a European airline with a financial interest in and technical association with the Thai airline is purely intentional.

THAI International, formed in 1959 through an agreement concluded between Thai Airways and SAS, took over all Thai overseas route licenses from May 1, 1960. Early advertising boasted of the association, touting 'SAS-captained Douglas aircraft'.

Two years later, THAI International began jet service with one of SAS's unwanted Coronados, but this proved too large and was replaced by...

...Caravelles from January 2, 1964. *Thepsatri* indicates, with the 'In Co-Operation With SAS' legend on the fuselage, that the relationship remained unchanged.

THAI International's use of the Caravelle was an early example of what today is called ETOPS (Extended Twin Operations), flying over the South China Sea between Hong Kong and Manila, and over the East China Sea from Taipei to Osaka. Although segments were modest by current standards, it was the first use of a twin-jet on such routes, and indeed in all of Asia.

For its glamorous 'Royal Orchid' service, the airline outfitted the French lady with a relatively luxurious 2-2 layout (in both first- and economy-classes), for a total of only 72 seats. From 1966, Caravelles took over from the DC-6Bs entirely , thus making THAI International the region's first 'all-jet' airline.

The 18th Caravelle ordered by SAS, delivered in September 1960 as Knud Viking, this Series III was the second SE 210 leased to THAI International, from March 1964 until October 1970. Returned to SAS for another four years of service in Europe, OY-KRE (renamed Gaut Viking) last flew on September 18, 1974. After use by Stockholm-Arlanda's fire department, it was broken up in October 1977.

One of three Model 30A-5s (990As) built for American Airlines but acquired by Garuda, Sriwijaja *was one of two sold to California Airmotive Corp in June 1973, after several years of storage at Jakarta. Refurbished at Hong Kong by HAECO and re-registered N7876, it crashed at Guam on September 10, 1973, while on delivery to the USA.*

The Indonesian airline Garuda preferred American-built equipment, at least the large jets, and became one of the relatively small number of airlines to operate the Convair 990A in scheduled service.

Garuda (named after a legendary bird-like creature) purchased three 990As to replace Lockheed Electra turboprops which, in 1961, had extended its Manila service to Hong Kong and Tokyo. Service with the new type–to Tokyo–started in September 1963, and it also inaugurated the airline's first service to Europe–to Amsterdam–18 months later. During their six years with Garuda, the 990s flew more than 25,000 hours.

Garuda also used a single example of the DC-8-55, named *Siliwangi*, seen here receiving a windshield polish before returning to Jakarta. A second aircraft, also ordered in August 1965, was never delivered and was taken over by KLM.

In a reversal of colonial ties, this aircraft went to KLM after three years service with the Indonesian airline and was replaced with two DC-8-33s leased from the Dutch company. These Garuda/KLM Eights replaced the uneconomical 990As on services to Amsterdam via Cairo and Rome, and opened service to Sydney in November 1969.

PK-GJD was leased by Douglas to Overseas National Airways (as N2310B) for one month before delivery to Garuda in July 1966. Transferred to KLM in March 1969 as PH-DCY, it operated in Garuda/Martinair colors, then as KLM's Anthony Fokker, before returning to GA in May 1973 as PK-GJD (re-registered PK-GEA a year later). Retired in April 1980, it eventually found its way back to the US as N225VV. In 1995, now a freighter, it was active with the Miami-based Fine Airlines, although registered in Colombia as HK-3753X.

SSSR-76490 is believed to have been the last of 36 Tu-114s built between 1957 and 1961. Most aircraft have now been scrapped, but '490 is displayed at the Museum of Civil Aviation, Ulyanovsk.

After a lengthy delay, in January 1967 the Soviet Union and Japan came to an agreement for starting a service between Moscow and Tokyo, overflying Siberia, and thus offering the shortest distance service between Europe and the Far East.

Aeroflot's massive Tupolev Tu-114 served on the route, flown weekly from April 17, 1967, and clearly advertised the joint operation by displaying the *Tsuru* emblem and JAL titles on the forward fuselage. The aircraft operated with a flight crew of six–five from Aeroflot and one JAL advisor–and a cabin crew of ten, including three stewardesses from each airline. Accommodation was for 44 first- and 72 economy-class passengers. The previous flight time was cut from more than 19 hours to 10hr 35min eastbound and 11hr 50min westbound.

Eventually, the Tu-114s gave way to Aeroflot Il-62s, then JAL operated its own flights over the trans-Siberia route from March 1970.

A more unusual Soviet visitor to Haneda in the unsociable 'sixties was this Ilyushin Il-18 which appears to have arrived on a diplomatic mission. Judging from the window layout, this aircraft has a three-cabin interior, with seating for between 73 and 111 persons (the number of seats could also vary depending on the season because of the passengers' heavy winter clothing).

A contemporary of the Lockheed Electra, the 100-seat Il-18 was built in far greater numbers: 569 versus 170 for the US type, and–like the Burbank-built turboprop–the Moscow (Khodinka)-constructed propliner was also produced in specialist military versions.

Il-18V SSSR-75742 was built in 1961, the second aircraft in the 28th production batch. Its final fate is not confirmed, but it is presumed to have been scrapped.

Delivered new to TAI in April 1955, F-BHEE became part of the UTA fleet in October 1963. Two years later it was sold to Iran Air as EP-AEX. US company Bird Air, based at Oakland, California, but a southeast Asia CIA-affiliated operator, acquired the DC-6B in October 1974 as N56CA, but a year later it was retired at Seletar, Singapore, and subsequently scrapped.

In addition to the plethora of scheduled services, as we have seen, Tokyo also was a popular destination for charters. Future UTA (Union de Transports Aériens) component, TAI (Transports Aériens Intercontinentaux), provides a 60-seat 'Super' DC-6B in 1961 as evidence of a French connection in this respect.

At the time, TAI claimed a round-the-world service from Paris via Tahiti, also stopping at Rangoon, Bangkok, Phnom Penh, Saigon, and Djakarta, but completed the Los Angeles–Paris sector thanks to Air France.

Another example of a Douglas product in the same circumstance is seen in the form of a Balair DC-4. Formed in 1948 as a flying school, this Basle (Basel)-Mulhouse-based company did not start airline operations until 1957 when it acquired Vickers Vikings. (The first Balair–Basler Luftverkehr–had started service in 1926 and was merged with Ad Astra five years later to form Swissair.)

Subsequently, Swissair took a financial interest and DC-4s were acquired in 1959. As well as European and worldwide charters, Balair also flew scheduled services on behalf of Swissair and operated for the Red Cross and United Nations. The Swiss flag carrier's subsidiary would be noted as one of the last operators of a Douglas four piston-engined airliner in Europe, with a DC-6B active as late as 1982.

After spending a colorful postwar career with Trans Caribbean Airways, Eastern, Near East Air Transport, Seaboard & Western Airlines, Los Angeles Air Service (Kirk Kekorian), Meteor Air Transport, General, Atlas, and American International Airways, this C-54A was acquired by Balair in December 1960. Sold to Air Ferry in January 1964 as G-ASOG, it crashed on approach to Frankfurt three years later, on January 21.

Ex-Eastern Air Lines and US Navy C-54B/R5D-2 LN-SUP was bought by Braathens SAFE in November 1956. In April 1959, Norse Commander *had the distinction of operating the first commercial air service to Spitsbergen. Sold to Transportflug, Germany, as D-ADAR. it was stored by August 1968, and later scrapped.*

Another Four appears here: *Norse Commander* is under the aegis of Norway's Braathens SAFE Airtransport. The acronym was not a reference to the dependability of the carrier, but stood for South American and Far East, destinations it had served from Norway on a charter and scheduled basis from 1947.

As the Braathens-operated Oslo–Hong Kong scheduled route conflicted with the ideals of the Scandinavian Airlines System's consortium, in 1954 the license was not renewed and the shipping company's subsidiary then concentrated on scheduled domestic routes and worldwide charters.

Weighing in with yet another Douglas is Transair of Sweden. This time the aircraft is a 'straight' Six. Sharp looking in its natural metal/red livery, only the registration hints that the aircraft is leased from SABENA.

Malmö-based Transair Sweden AB operated IT (inclusive tour) charters for Swedish, Danish, Swiss, and German travel agencies, and undertook charters with passengers and freight all over the world, plus domestic night mail services. It was also active in the Belgian Congo, flying for the United Nations. Three DC-6s were acquired from SAS in 1959, and two from SABENA to add to its Curtiss C-46 and DC-3 fleet.

Built in 1950, DC-6 OO-SDE (formerly OO-AWW) was leased to El Al and Liberian International besides Transair Sweden during its 15-year career with SABENA. Purchased by Air Congo (later Air Zaïre) in July 1965 as 9Q-CLB, it was withdrawn from use about 1970 and later scrapped.

Built for Slick Airways in 1953, DC-6A N90809 was sold to Hawaiian Airlines five years later and named King Kamehameha–The Pacific Adventurer. Because of the termination of military contracts, Hawaiian leased the aircraft to Finlantic between October 1961 and March 1963. Two years later, it was parked at Honolulu and the following year sold to Mitsui in trade for YS-11As. After passing through the hands of several brokers, it was sold to Ecuatoriana in September 1970 as HC-ATR. Finally retired five years later, it was broken up at Quito early in the 1980s.

Another Nordic entrant is this well-traveled 98-seat DC-6A of Finlantic, probably operating a seamen's charter. Sorry, no prizes given for identification of this carrier's nationality. Finlantic was formed in 1961 to take advantage of the increasing IT charter traffic from overcast northern European skies to the azure blue of the Mediterranean. (At the time, International Air Transport Association-member airlines were prohibited from carrying such traffic, although most simply formed non-IATA subsidiaries to overcome this handicap.)

Very soon Finlantic found itself competing with the state-owned airline, after Finnair took over control of Kar-Air, and it ceased operations early in 1963.

It should be apparent from the spelling of the name that this operator is not based in an English-speaking country. The registration–applied later to a Lufthansa Boeing 737–provides another helpful hint.

This Skymaster is a good example of the cosmetic disguise, in the form of square window outlines painted on the fuselage, that a number of airlines used to try to convince casual viewers that the aircraft was a DC-6–a pressurized airplane–instead of an earlier, unpressurized DC-4.

Hamburg-based Continentale Deutsche Luftreederei GmbH started non-scheduled operations in June 1959, and specialized in charter flights to the Middle and Far East, and Africa.

This ex-USAAF C-54B-DC had been The Gates of Suez *(N86571) with TWA from 1946 until 1958, when it was acquired by Eastern Aircraft Sales and operated by Aerotour Deutsche Luftreederei as D-ADEM, then D-AKIR, under a lease-purchase contract. Following the collapse of Aerotour in December 1958, the aircraft was repossessed by Eastern and sold to Continentale. It was lost in the airline's only accident, on approach to Kano, Nigeria, on June 17, 1961.*

Destined to become a Carvair, this C-54B was converted to civilian standard by Douglas and delivered to Western Air Lines in 1946. Moving across the North Atlantic to SOBELAIR of Belgium as OO-SBO ten years later, it passed on to Continentale Deutsche Luftreederei in 1960. Transformed into an ATL 98 in 1963, it enjoyed another 11 years of service with Aer Lingus, Eastern Provincial Airways, and British Air Ferries. In 1974, it was sold to Norwegian Overseas Airways for relief work in Asia, and was eventually parked at Bangkok where it was broken up.

Although another Skymaster with the German charter airline appeared in a different paint scheme–a leftover from the previous operator–the concern about putting round holes in square outlines seems to have continued unabated.

Continentale first used two DC-4s previously operated by Hamburg-based Aerotour Deutsche Luftreederei which had lasted about a year and had itself been formed from the ashes of Columbus Luftreederei, yet another 'non-sked' which hailed from the free Hansa port on the Elbe. A dedicated DC-4 operator (it used a total of five), Continentale did not benefit from its one-type fleet and, following its predecessors, went into voluntary liquidation in December 1962.

As we saw in *Skyliners 2*, a number of Italian propliners had registration suffixes whose four letters formed English words; perhaps I-DIME was a reference to stopping capability, or turning radius, (In reality, this one was part of an alphabet soup running from -MA to -MU, but someone with a sense of humor was responsible for registering those in the series whose leading letter was Lima, which included, among eight DC-6s, LADY, LIKE, LOVE, LUCK and LYNX, with no intervening non-word examples.)

While subtly different, it is not hard to see a family resemblance between the liveries of non-IATA charter subsidiary SAM (Societa Aerea Mediterranea), shown here, and its parent flag carrier ALITALIA (Aerolinee Italiane Internazionali). Note also the 'Italia 61' sticker, a tourist promotion theme.

I-DIME was delivered to ALITALIA in January 1954, then passed to SAM in April 1961. Damaged eight years later in a landing accident at Bari, it recovered to become MM61987 with the Aeronautica Militare Italiane (Italian Air Force) in July 1970, assigned to the Reparto Volo Stato Maggiore at Rome-Ciampino for VIP duties and coded SM-29. Retired in 1974 with the delivery of DC-9s, the DC-6B was eventually scrapped at Venice.

Built for BOAC, this Hermes IVA (Bristol Hercules 773 engines burning 100 octane fuel) was not accepted by the Corporation and instead was delivered to Airwork Ltd in October 1952. In 1957, it reverted to Mark IV standard (Hercules 763, 115 octane fuel) and in October 1959, was acquired by a new UK independent, Blackbushe-based Falcon Airways. After just one year, it passed to Air Safaris, followed in quick succession to Skyways, then Air Links, which converted it to an 82-seater. On December 13, 1964, G-ALDA completed the last revenue flight of a Hermes when it landed at Gatwick; it was scrapped at Southend the following year.

This sleek propliner is notable on two counts, first in being one of 25 Handley Page Hermes IVs built, and in its representation of the relatively brief career of British charter company Falcon Airways.

Falcon was formed in March 1959 by Polish-born Capt Marian Kozubski, who had been managing director of Independent Air Transport, another British airline. Two Hermes joined a Vickers Viking that summer, but were disposed of in favor of Constellations at the end of the following year. Although the airline flew mostly IT holiday charters to the Mediterranean, occasional forays were made to North America and, as here in May 1960, to Tokyo.

After numerous battles with the UK civil aviation authorities which led to the loss of several contracts, Falcon ceased operations in September 1961.

Another British IT operation during the same time period was that of Overseas Aviation, which used nine Canadair C-4 Argonauts (a reference to the type's class name with BOAC) and picked up nine similar DC-4M North Stars from Trans-Canada Air Lines plus, from the same source, two ex-Canadian Pacific C-4s. Coincidentally, the Rolls-Royce Merlin-powered DC-4 variants were the type which had supplanted the Hermes IV at BOAC, from which Overseas had obtained its original fleet.

Formed by Ronald Myhill, who had previously founded Autair, LTU (Germany), and Aviameer (Belgium), Gatwick-based Overseas lasted a little longer than Falcon, from 1957 to 1961. During its final season it operated the second largest fleet, after British United, of any British independent operator.

Flown by BOAC with the name Aurora *from 1949, C-4 G-ALHG was sold to Overseas Aviation in 1960. Eighteen months later, in October 1961, the Argonaut passed to Derby Airways, which was renamed British Midland three years later. Hotel Golf was destroyed in a fatal accident on approach to Manchester-Ringway on June 4, 1967.*

Built as a DC-8-32 in 1960, JA8005 was later upgraded to a -33. After 14 years with JAL, it was sold to American Jet Industries in May 1974 and re-registered N421AJ. Two years later, it was converted to a freighter and served with Evergreen International, Rosenbalm, Zantop International, and Emery Worldwide. In the mid-1908s, it moved to Africa as 5N-AYZ with International Air Tours (International Airline Support Group), then to São Tomé–based Transafrik as S9-NAB. It was broken up at Johannesburg in October 1989, just a few flights shy of 50,000 hours.

Miyajima is participating in some event out of the ordinary. Photographer Mel Lawrence's caption on the slide mount ('Emperor returns from Sapporo') certainly sheds some light on the situation. Emperor Hirohito's arrival at his home city's airport serves to remind us that the time has come to consider returning home as well.

Airways... the exciting international bi-monthly magazine devoted to airlines and commercial aircraft. Flying them, operating them, traveling in them, supporting them. The manufacturers, the operators, the people, the new technology, the airports and the airways. Plus a nostalgic look at the past.

Written for airline and air travel industry professionals and aficionados, **Airways** features quality editorial written by those with a genuine and comprehensive background in the airline and air transport industry. All supported by the very best photography and a vast database of research material.

For Subscription info:
Call TOLL-FREE +1 800 440 5166
Outside USA: +1 208 263 2098
or Fax: +1 208 263 5906

Airways International, Inc.
PO Box 1109
Sandpoint, ID 83864, USA
Tel: +1 208 263 2098
Fax: +1 208 263 5906

Airways International, Ltd.
14 Fawcett Crescent
Woodley, RG5 3HU, England
Tel: +44 1734 694626
Fax: +44 1734 440576

A GLOBAL REVIEW OF COMMERCIAL FLIGHT

Airways
Nov/Dec 1994

Everyone
Versus
Southwest

Hollywood and
the Airlines

AOM French
Airlines

US $3.95 • Canada $5.95

0 73361 64595 1   11

Coming soon...
SKYLINERS4